Praise

Diaries of an Unfini

'If ever there is a book that should be championed, it is [*Diaries of an Unfinished Revolution*]. . . . Among the most moving, inspiring, and revealing pieces of non-fiction we've come across in some time.'
— *The National* (UAE)

'[This book] provides a terrifying insight into the world of authoritarian regimes where freedom and democracy are alien concepts. Each of the eight accounts in this impressive anthology is accessible and illuminating.'
— *The Independent* (UK)

'[*Diaries of an Unfinished Revolution*] is not the revolution itself, but its continuation with literary means. As people in the Arab world recaptured the public sphere, this book opens a literary space, in which the actors and authors of the revolutions can meet and express free of fear. It is a book that nobody can avoid if he wants to understand what is happening in the Arab world.'
— *Diesseits*

'What this anthology makes abundantly clear is that the young people behind these uprisings, though often optimistic, were not blinded by the fervour of revolution but were in fact acutely aware of the obstacles that lay ahead.'
— *London School of Economics Review of Books*

'These accounts . . . [offer] examples of heroism and of hope for the future.'
—Samar Yazbek, author of *A Woman in the Crossfire*, from the Introduction to this book

DIARIES OF AN UNFINISHED REVOLUTION

VOICES FROM TUNIS TO DAMASCUS

EDITED BY LAYLA AL-ZUBAIDI,
MATTHEW CASSEL **AND**
NEMONIE CRAVEN RODERICK

TRANSLATED BY ROBIN MOGER AND GEORGINA COLLINS
WITH AN INTRODUCTION BY SAMAR YAZBEK

PENGUIN BOOKS

PENGUIN BOOKS

Published by the Penguin Group
Penguin Group (USA) LLC, 375 Hudson Street, New York, New York 10014

USA I Canada I UK I Ireland I Australia I New Zealand I India I South Africa I China
penguin.com
A Penguin Random House Company

First published in Great Britain as *Writing Revolution: The Voices from Tunis to Damascus* by
I.B. Tauris & Co. Ltd. 2013
First published in the United States of America as *Diaries of an Unfinished Revolution: Voices
from Tunis to Damascus* in Penguin Books 2013

This book was produced with financial support from Heinrich Böll Stiftung. The views
expressed herein are, however, solely those of the authors.

▐▌▌ HEINRICH BÖLL STIFTUNG
MIDDLE EAST

LIBRARY OF CONGRESS CATALOGING-IN-PUBLICATION DATA
Diaries of an unfinished revolution : voices from Tunis to Damascus / edited by Layla Al-
Zubaidi, Matthew Cassel, and Nemonie Craven Roderick ; translated by Robin Moger and
Georgina Collins ; introduction by Samar Yazbek.
pages cm
ISBN 978-0-14-312515-0 (pbk.)
1. Arab Spring, 2010—Personal narratives.   2. Political rights—Arab countries.
3. Revolutionary literature.   4. Protest literature.   I. Al-Zubaidi, Layla, editor of
compilation.   II. Cassel, Matthew (Matthew E.), editor of compilation.
III. Roderick, Nemonie Craven.   IV. Title.
JQ1850.A91.W75 2013
323'.04409174927—dc23   2013030333

Printed in the United States of America
10 9 8 7 6 5 4 3 2 1

CONTENTS

PREFACE

Many of us would like to think that we experienced the 2011 uprisings in the Arab world first-hand. It was magical to watch events unfold live on TV and computer screens, across the world. As fast and as often as we could, we tweeted and facebooked articles, pictures, updates, anything to spread the word and feel involved.

For those on the ground in the Arab world, however, these events had been long in the making. Activists such as Jamal Jubran in Yemen didn't need to wait for the international media to become comfortable with calling a dictator a 'dictator' to understand the true oppressiveness of certain governments. As he writes in his essay 'The Resistance: Armed with Words': 'Words were my weapons.' Before the spotlight focused on these despots and the massive protests against them, countless people had already sacrificed everything to challenge their absolute rule.

What we witnessed on television was only a small part of a larger struggle that didn't begin with the self-immolation of Tunisian fruitseller Mohamed Bouazizi, or end when one dictator took a plane to Saudi and another a bullet to the head. And as people took to the streets, the same media that, for so long, had failed to highlight Egypt's dungeons or Bahrain's protests or Tunisia's sham elections, now covered the Arab world on its front pages. As the young Libyan writer Mohamed

Mesrati remarks in the pages that follow: 'Those in the Libyan diaspora began seeing images of Libya in the local and international press – headlines that talked not of Gaddafi but of ordinary Libyans. In the newsagents I stood dazed before the serried ranks of newsprint.'

At times there was a clear effort made to engage people on the ground, but the dominant voices discussing the uprisings in most English-language media came from an elite group of professional 'experts', often commenting far from the battles taking place in the streets. This book aims to correct that.

The contributors to this anthology did not sit on the sidelines while things happened. Each of them played a role in shaping their country's future and documenting uncomfortable truths long before the wave of mass uprisings began, and they continue to do so, even when events fall out of the headlines. And because of their involvement, obtaining their contribution was not always an easy task.

Ali Abdulemam, the Bahraini blogger and rights activist, who quickly joined protests in Manama in February 2011, having only that same month been released from a prison sentence which started in September 2010, was amongst the first to agree to contribute to this project. During a crackdown on dozens of activists, politicians, writers and others, in June 2011 he was sentenced, in absentia, to 15 years in prison. Ali had gone into hiding before he could be arrested once more and we received no word from him for over two years – until he emerged in May 2013 in the UK, where he has been granted asylum. Dr Ali Aldairy, an accomplished Bahraini journalist and author whose story you will read in this book, only picked up a pen again when he safely made it out of the country in 2011, entering a life of exile away from home.

Malek Sghiri, on the other hand, is a young Tunisian student whom we met in March 2011 in Tunis. He had led student marches in Tunis, fought against the security forces in his hometown of Tala, and was detained and tortured in the infamous prisons of the Interior Ministry on Bourguiba Avenue, while thousands of protesters outside cheered the news that Ben Ali had fled the country. After he was released he continued to be active, in particular around issues of youth representation. At a conference in Tunis on the Arab revolutions, he criticized older speakers for limiting speaking time for younger delegates. 'Don't patronize the youth as our dictators have done for decades!' he said. Today, Malek is a writer and one of the student leaders involved in working towards maintaining the goals of the revolution.

Syrian journalist Khawla Dunia came to our attention in April 2011, through her regular contributions to the influential website *Safhat Suriya* (Syrian Pages), one of the few that features uncensored opinion. When phoning her in order to ask her for a contribution, we avoided using words like 're-volution' or 'activism' since calls are often monitored in Syria and could lead to arrests. During an awkward conversation trying to explain the project in coded language, she inter-rupted: 'You want to know why I'm engaged in the revolution? Because it's about our dignity. This is also why I will speak with you on the phone as I please and I will write as I please.' Khawla has emerged as one of the most poignant Syrian voices and as a tireless activist for the displaced, providing shelter and humanitarian aid. By evoking the early civil protests and activism on the ground, her account provides important documentation of the beginnings of the Syrian uprising – now buried under headlines about civil war and geo-political endgames.

All the contributors to this book have affected or been affected by the course of events in their countries: whether they have faced years of harassment from the authorities, like Jamal Jubran in Sanaa; or by giving voice to their country's stories on international platforms, like Egyptian Yasmine El Rashidi. The personal narrative of Saudi Safa Al Ahmad particularly stresses how political repression and the oppression and silencing of women are intertwined. Ghania Mouffok has been a critical voice in Algeria for many years; Mohamed Mesrati is a young, talented writer living in the UK since 2005 as a result of his family's persecution under Gaddafi.

The contributors to this book are writers and thinkers engaged in a process of deep personal and political reflection. For most of them, it is the first time their work has been published in English translation. This is a unique collection of testimony: situated between past, present and future – in a space where the personal and the political meet – these voices are bound to an ongoing process.

Our aim, as editors, was to put the narrative of 'the Arab Spring' back into the hands of the people without whom there would be no story to tell.

Layla Al-Zubaidi, Matthew Cassel
and Nemonie Craven Roderick
June, 2013

ACKNOWLEDGEMENTS

Layla Al-Zubaidi, Matthew Cassel and Nemonie Craven Roderick would like to thank the following, whose support made this book possible:

The Heinrich Böll Foundation, especially Corinne Deek and Hiba Haidar; Nadine El-Hadi and I.B.Tauris; Robert Sharp and English PEN; Ali Abdulemam, Pierre Abi Saab, Fatema Abuidrees, Ali Alizadeh, Amira Chebli, Ahmed Habib, Mustafa Haid, Yasmeen El Khoudary, Robin Moger, Afrah Nasser, Moe Ali Nayel, Ayesha Saldanha, Mona Seif, Ala'a Shehabi, Haroon Shirwani, Hussein Yaakoub and Rami Zurayk.

CONTRIBUTORS

Editors

Layla Al-Zubaidi is Director of the Heinrich Böll Foundation in South Africa, and was previously based in Beirut and Ramallah. She has published on cultural resistance and freedom of expression, and is co-editor of *Democratic Transition in the Middle East: Unmaking Power* (Routledge, 2012). She is also on the Executive Committee of Freemuse – World Forum on Music and Censorship.

Matthew Cassel is a journalist and photographer covering the Middle East for *Al Jazeera English*. Matthew first learned about the region through his human rights and media work in Palestinian refugee camps. Over the past decade he has worked in the occupied Palestinian territories, Lebanon, Egypt, Turkey, Syria, Jordan, Bahrain and elsewhere. Formerly Assistant Editor of the *The Electronic Intifada* online journal, he is connected to activists, journalists, writers, artists and others at the forefront of the movement for change in the region.

Nemonie Craven Roderick is a literary agent. She has contributed to *Sight & Sound*, *Roads & Kingdoms* and *The Blackwell Encyclopedia of Literary and Cultural Theory*, amongst other publications.

Authors

Ali Aldairy is a Bahraini researcher, linguist and cultural critic, interested in philosophy and religion. He is the author of several books. A long-standing activist, he has been struggling since the Bahraini uprising in 2011 and was forced to leave the country. In exile he founded the online Arabic newspaper *Mira'at al-Bahrain* (*The Bahrain Mirror*).

Safa Al Ahmad is a Saudi freelance journalist based in the Middle East. She has worked both in print and for TV, for major channels in the region, and was a finalist for the 2012 Rory Peck awards for freelance journalism. With the start of the second intifada she travelled to Palestine, then on to Lebanon, Bahrain, the Democratic Republic of Congo and Libya, among other places. Her film *Al Qaeda in Yemen* was nominated for an Emmy Award in 2013.

Khawla Dunia is a lawyer, writer and researcher and a member of the editorial board of The Damascus Center for Theoretical Studies and Civil Rights. She has published several studies, including *Syrian Women between Reality and Ambition*, *Report on the Damascus Declaration Detainees* and reports on elections and political issues. Khawla is now active in the protests and writes about them on the Arabic website *Safhat Suriya* (*Syria Pages*).

Yasmine El Rashidi is a frequent contributor to the *New York Review of Books*, and a contributing editor to the Middle East arts and culture quarterly *Bidoun*. A collection of her writings on the Egyptian uprising, *The Battle for Egypt*, was published in 2011. She lives in Cairo.

Jamal Jubran is a journalist, poet and author, based in Sanaa. He regularly contributes to Beirut-based *Al-Akhbar* and his articles have been translated and published in a number of international publications. He has also taught at Sanaa University, but was expelled because of his political activities. Before and during the Yemeni uprising, he was active in the group around Nobel Peace Prize laureate Tawakkol Karman.

Mohamed Mesrati was born in 1990 in Tripoli, Libya. He is a writer and activist, and an extract from his novel-in-progress *Mama Pizza* appeared in *Banipal No. 40*.

Ghania Mouffok is a journalist based in Algiers. She is a correspondent for *TV5MONDE* and hosts the blog *Une femme à sa fenêtre* on the channel's website. She writes for various journals, including *Le Monde Diplomatique*, the Swiss *La Liberté*, and the Algerian online-journal *Maghreb Émergent*. Ghania is also an engaged feminist and human rights activist and collaborates with the UN and civil society organizations. Among her publications are *Une autre voie pour l'Algérie* (with Louisa Hanoune, 1995), *Être journaliste en Algérie* (1996) and *Apprendre à vivre ensemble* (2011).

Malek Sghiri was born in 1987 and is a student of Contemporary History at the April 9 Faculty of Human and Social Sciences in Tunis. He is a political activist, blogger, trade unionist and leader of the General Union of Tunisian Students. Malek founded the movement Jil Jadid (New Generation), participated in student demonstrations in Tunis, in the revolt of Tala, and in the mass protests against the rule of Ben Ali that took place in Tadamon. He was arrested and detained at the Ministry of Interior on 11 January and later released on 18 January 2011.

Samar Yazbek is a Syrian writer and journalist. She was born in Jableh in 1970, in northwestern Syria, and was forced into exile following her criticism of the al-Assad regime and involvement in the Syrian uprising. In 2012, she won the PEN/ Pinter International Writer of Courage prize for her book *A*

Woman in the Crossfire and the PEN Tucholsky prize in Sweden. Samar is soon to be awarded the PEN OXFAM prize in the Netherlands. She is the author of numerous works of fiction and was selected as one of the *Beirut39* in 2010.

Translators

Robin Moger is an Arabic translator currently living in Cape Town, South Africa. From 2001 to 2007 he lived in Egypt, where he worked variously as a journalist, translator and interpreter. He is the translator of two novels – *A Dog With No Tail* by Hamdi Abu Gollayel (2009) and *Vertigo* by Ahmed Mourad (2011). Robin also regularly contributes to *Banipal*, the magazine of modern Arab literature.

Georgina Collins is a lecturer in Translation Studies at the University of Glasgow. She researches the translation of Francophone postcolonial literature and also works as a freelance translator. Georgina also published the first anthology of Francophone African women's poetry, *The Other Half of History*, featuring her own translations into English.

Note on Transliteration

Arabic names and terms are loosely transliterated. The most common spelling is used for widely-known names and terms.

INTRODUCTION

By Samar Yazbek
Translated from the Arabic by Robin Moger

Writing about revolution is not easy. It poses a moral dilemma: what is the validity of any endeavour that takes place outside the ferment of the revolution itself? Is silence and activism preferable? Or can writing also be a valid form of engagement, though it entails occasionally stepping back from the reality on the ground? These are painful questions, leading to choices whose outcome cannot be guaranteed. History tells us that many of the greatest works on revolution were written by authors who were never at the centre of events, who stood at the margins or who watched from afar.

Ours is a time in which the profession of writing is deeply bound up with that of political activism, especially now that Facebook and Twitter and all the other online platforms have made writing so much more effective. In this new environment, priority is given to the rapid reporting and assimilation of unfolding events; what is important is then filtered out, and a space for debate is created, in which public opinion might take form. This new environment shaped these revolutions from their outset and it signals the end of the classical conception of the writer, of his or her traditionally recognized role and influence. Writing is now for everyone, and the short texts shared on the pages of Facebook activists have become important documents. These revolutions pre-empted the process of revolutionary and intellectual theorizing, and yet now wait on a new form of literature to describe them: a writing forged in the present moment.

The accounts in this book offer us a profound insight into the condition in which these societies lived, burdened as they were by dictatorships dressed up as civil bureaucracies. They identify these societies' terminal weaknesses and flaws and show us that the changes which lie ahead will be yet more demanding.

Khawla Dunia writes about Syria. Her testimony is important for the light it sheds on people's decisions to take to the streets and to demand freedom and dignity. Khawla is a former political prisoner with an interest in public affairs and culture, and her account is an example of the interplay of subjective experience and objective reportage that runs through this book – the personal all but pushed out in favour of the daily events she recounts. The situation in Syria is tragic because it is the bloodiest of the revolutions. It is as if she has been writing a history of the democratic opposition in Syria, only for the revolution to sweep her up. It is easier to pick up the thread of unfolding events on the ground than it is to access the subjective experiences of a woman who has worked in the civil society movement from the first days of the revolution – which Khawla continues to do, even after the Syrian security services began to pursue her. In the first days of the revolution, Khawla began to write poetry. What happened in Syria led her to rediscover herself. She is no longer just a woman who works in politics: now she is a poet, too.

Jamal Jubran's experiences in Yemen have a different feel. They celebrate the personal and the existential with impressive and affecting delicacy. They are a vivid and human account of the persecution he lived through from before the revolution to the present day. His own suffering is part of the experience of all Yemenis who lived under the dictatorship of Ali Abdullah Saleh. The value of what Jamal has written lies in his talent as a journalist of the first rank, introduced early to the world of press and politics. He writes honestly about his position on the fringe of the revolution, clearly stating that though not at the heart of events he has done all he could to be with and of them, and this he has achieved. He talks to us with precision and skill and with sadness, too, but not without a glimmer of optimism. This is a piece of autobiography, one of exceptional literary merit.

From Bahrain, Ali Aldairy tells, with considerable anger, his story and that of his country's ignored revolution, of which the world knows little as a result of a near total media blackout from international and Arab news organizations. But Ali's story is different. He makes clear how the situation has left foreign observers baffled, with some calling it a revolution of the Shia against the rule of the Sunni al-Khalifa and others describing it as an uprising, a revolution of the poor and marginalized against the plutocratic ruling class. He explains his rage against the intellectuals who pretend neutrality but show no empathy with the pain and injustice suffered by the people. He engages with the profound existential question of the intellectual's proper role – as opposed to what we too often see: cowardice and reluctance to stand with the people. The real and vital duty of the intellectual is to change society and this is what many of Bahrain's intellectuals have failed to do. Ali makes all this clear by recounting his own personal experiences and his piece is filled with pain.

Mohamed Mesrati artfully portrays Libya under the dictatorship through the story of his own family, which was forced to leave the country for opposing Muammar Gaddafi's regime. He weaves an enchanting tale of his relationship with his childhood friends and his desire to return to his country during the revolution. For Mohamed, writing about Libya's revolution is a homecoming, a re-joining; when he speaks about contributing through social media or his mother's political activism he is trying to tell us that this is where he comes from: from the heart of the revolution. Perhaps this is his response to the issue of identity, which troubles the sleep of so many displaced and exiled Arabs scattered across the world. But Mohamed blends his dream of becoming a famous writer with another revolutionary dream of Libya's transformation into a civil democracy, both dreams swirling into one another.

From Tunisia and its Jasmine revolution, Malek Sghiri speaks of being a student activist. He was raised on politics. His father was imprisoned for seven years and he has inherited the struggle from a family that has been involved in political opposition for a century. What may be most valuable in Malek's account is the detail he provides of the Tunisian student movement and its role in the revolution, which he conveys to us through his own highly personal account: he does not hold back from talking of love, of the beatings he received, of his kidnapping, imprisonment and detention. The revolution does not end with Ben Ali's departure, but rather, it begins anew, with the figureheads from the old regime trying to regain power. The revolution and the protests go on; the struggle continues.

Malek makes no attempt to hide his pain, or his hope that the true leadership created by the revolution will now emerge: it is his firmly held belief that those who deserve most credit for shaping the revolution never gained the recognition due to them. Here we see a stark contradiction and a source of disappointment: the gulf between his romantic revolutionary dreams and the reality of a popular, rebellious revolution issuing forth from the throats of the people, now consigned to the hushed corridors and meeting rooms of conferences, ministries and television studios. He reveals that it is too early to pronounce the revolution a success; that the revolution in Tunisia continues. What matters, is that his experience has honed him and enabled him to engage in his work in the student movement with greater awareness and commitment.

Safa Al Ahmad's piece from Saudi Arabia seems to summarize the experience of all the revolutions in its account of the protests in Qatif that were ruthlessly suppressed, and the general complicity against the protest movement. There are some things that can lose you your head in Saudi Arabia, but even so people scrawled 'Death to al-Saud' on the walls and the protest movement kept going, especially amongst the Shia who supported the revolution in Bahrain. Women in Saudi Arabia are still forbidden from driving cars, a crime punishable by law. How can a revolution take root in such circumstances? Saudi Arabia's experience is painful, bitter and desperate but it is one that must be explored. Despite international complicity, despite the difficulty and danger of holding a successful revolution against a monarchy backed by the Americans and the other Gulf states, there is still hope, though it may take time.

Algeria has a sad and bitter history of aborted uprisings against the status quo. It began long before the current wave of revolutions in the Arab world and met an equally premature end in the 1990s, bringing great misery to Algerian society. It is significant that this testimony should be written by a woman, Ghania Mouffok, since Algerian women have suffered from the rise of Islamic fundamentalism; even more significant that the woman in question is a mother and journalist. She writes about contemporary Algerian history, the tales and the tragedies, the people who set themselves alight to escape their suffering, but she offers us a description, not a solution. Like others, she follows the course of events in her country full of fear and yearning.

Yasmine El Rashidi speaks of the Egyptian revolution, also through the prism of personal experience. She describes events with great precision; describes her life before the revolution and how it paved the way for her involvement in mass rebellion. She writes about the protests, her participation in the revolution, her family and, as the other authors have shown, the personal here only serves to illuminate the mechanisms by which the revolution evolved. Her account is full of energy and uncertainty, full of yearning for the future, and highlights the importance of women's involvement in the revolution.

Indeed, half the authors featured in this book are women and with this is mind we should pause to consider the role they have played in events and what the future holds for them. What of the women who started these revolutions, who took part in them and gave their lives for them; the women who were arrested, raped, murdered and hunted down? How can women participate in revolutions whose outcomes appear even more damaging to their cause? This is what happened in Libya and Tunisia, and what is currently happening in Egypt, where an Islamist government is trying to roll back the tentative advances made by the Arab women who struggled to ensure their rights were constitutionally enshrined and to secure a life in which the law did not treat them as second-class citizens.

This is a hard question and, given the rivers of blood that still flow in Syria and to a lesser degree elsewhere, the answer is complicated. We have reached a particularly difficult, but necessary, phase. The struggles and conflicts taking place within these revolutions against established social and political systems must be endured because the end of a dictator does not mean that we are done. I believe that the fall of the dictators across the Arab world marks the start of the true revolution. It will be that much harder for women. They have had to fight the dictators and now, they must fight against the manifold forms of Islamic religious extremism that have emerged in reaction to the region's stillborn secularist movements. Events in Egypt prove that the revolutions continue even after regimes have been brought down.

We women face a real problem, one far greater than can be summarized in a few pages of text, but beyond doubt the place of women is going to be the most crucial and inflammatory issue in this post-dictatorial world. In any case, for these women moving forward is the only viable choice.

Through personal experience and human detail these testimonies give a sense of how the movements that became revolutions first began. Something exceptional happened in the Arab world: the elites and the street walked side by side. It may be a little hasty to pass final judgement on these Arab revolutions and the profound changes that they could yet generate across the world. The testimonies make it clear how popular uprising led to protest movements that in turn became revolutions. This latter stage of development initiated by the children of the middle classes, followers of a moderate, open-minded Islam or secularists. It proves that it was the street that came first, only for their efforts to be appropriated by these middle-class elites, and not the other way round; the conventional assumption that elites initiate change with the masses then racing to catch them up no longer applies.

They remain revolutions in progress, after all: in some countries they have toppled their dictators while in others the blood still flows. Then there are the countries ruled by religious monarchies where any change seems impossible to contemplate.

These accounts vary between the personal and the general, but all express a single point: that writing in a time of revolution is part of the process of change. Moving between the subjective and the dispassionate they offer us examples of heroism and of hope for the future.

GREETINGS TO THE DAWN

LIVING THROUGH THE BITTERSWEET REVOLUTION (TUNISIA)

By Malek Sghiri
Translated from the Arabic by Robin Moger

Tunisia and its twin

You could go mad. That is how living in my dear country, Tunisia, made me feel. I concluded, not entirely seriously, that every Tunisian who, like me, looked closely at the situation in his homeland must carry within him the seeds of such a madness: the early symptoms of a split personality.

From the outside all seemed fine and nothing was fine from within. Everything was beautiful, rosy and full of life and hope on television and the 8 o'clock news, in the papers and on the radio; advertising slots were full of laughing, attractive faces encouraging us to buy what we produced. But in the city streets and suburbs, in the villages and towns, all was sad and shocking: faces yellowed by the vicissitudes of fate, the evaporation of dreams. Hordes of police stood watch everywhere, observing the cries and groans of lost time, which stamped its tattoo across the lips and brows of this fine people.

It was a dreadful contradiction, one that you lived out in the fine grain of your existence: the conflict between the life you were told that you lived and the one you really did; between the Tunisia of the TV screens and official pronouncements and the Tunisia of crowded transport, cities of dust, nepotism and police repression; between the verdant Tunisia that sprang from the minds of the liars who sprawled over our bodies and the sad Tunisia whose sufferings we bore in our palms each morning as we dreamed of a dawn to come.

Whether luckily or unluckily, I became familiar with this contradiction from an early age, not because of any precocious awareness or formidable intellect on my part, but thanks to the small, happy family in which I was raised.

The family had come to Tunis in the mid-'80s from a long-forgotten town called Tala, a place on the edge, geographically and otherwise, with bitterly cold winters and scorching heat in summer. The family carried the curse of political opposition, perhaps as a result of some genetic flaw (my two grandfathers, Tayyib and Lazhar, were revolutionaries of the National Movement, their fathers were leading figures of the 1906 peasant uprising in Tala and they were all descendants of Ali Ben Ghadahom, the leader of the 1864 revolt against Med Sadok Bey). Whatever the case, we lacked immunity to the virus of revolution and resistance and it infected us all, uncles, aunts, sons and daughters, with exceptions that, of course, proved the rule.

Memory

My father was imprisoned for his political views on two separate occasions, a total of seven years, first between 1983 and 1985 under President Habib Bourguiba and again under President Zine el-Abidine Ben Ali between 1991 and 1996. My mother, who with my ailing grandmother and wonderful uncle, shouldered the burden of raising me, my brother Dhaffer and sister Sana'a, became withdrawn. In nostalgic moments that squeeze the heart I still remember my mother's radiant face as she, not yet 30, gathered up our things and told us to be brave and strong as we were getting ready to visit my father in jail.

We would wake at four in the morning, sometimes three or even earlier when the journey was particularly long. Prison visits taught us the map of Tunis and its byways. The regime punished both him and us by constantly moving him from one jail to another.

Truth be told, neither I, my mother or my sister, and certainly not my father, ever slept the night before for reasons my words are powerless to convey. Twisting and turning on the narrow bed that I never once complained about because I knew my mother could not afford to buy another, I would ask myself why I couldn't hug my father like other children. Why must I pay weekly visits to my own father surrounded by jostling crowds, policemen, and heavy sticks? Why, Lord, do we not get to go with our parents to the seaside, the zoo or the funfair? Why don't we stay up watching TV, like all the families we see on the TV: laughing and joking in a warm and lovely home? Why do I have to stay awake, sharpening my hearing to catch my mother's weeping, the choking sobs she does not want to wake us with, while knowing that my siblings and I are listening in, our senses straining and our hearts catching at the sound?

Ah! How many times did my mother try to cover her mouth, I wonder, to protect us, or herself, from the torment of bitter wakefulness? How many times did my too-wide body flip on my narrow bed to my young thoughts and youthful questions?

I did not complain. I was raised on values that I imbibed with my mother's milk: courage, to bear the burden of a sacred trust; fortitude, to defy and overcome your baser self; honesty, to speak the truth when others fall silent; modesty, to turn your back on material wealth; manliness, to hold your head high when asked to bow before the storm; piety, to remain faithful to your parents; dignity, to pluck your right to live from the hands of your tormentors; and gallantry, to tread humbly.

These images and symbols were engraved on my consciousness and can never be erased: tears, a shaking hand, a sob stifled in the throat. I do not like to put my private self on display. I am not one of those who have no difficulty unburdening themselves to an audience, perhaps because I cannot control myself when I write or talk about even a part of this family life. I feel that I'm betraying those moments as I set them down: a distortion that robs them of their powerful presence in my life.

I remember every name, every date: everything. I remember every prison and every prison guard. I remember every entrance and exit, every visitor, every prisoner's face. I remember the chilly waiting rooms, the iron bars that kept me from my father, the little pieces of halva he held out to us across the metre that separated us from his warm embrace. I remember the train, the bus, the railway, the long road and utter silence that preceded our meeting with our father. I remember every detail and I do not have to pay the price of wringing my memory out to retrieve it. My memory is alive with these details; details that formed me as I am today. How can I forget how I am?

Taken together all these things formed part of my rage at the regime that fractured my family. I confess that I am angry and bitter at this regime and I confess that I wanted revenge, but I also confess, with a clear conscience, that the trifling things I did – which others call fighting for freedom and which I call the search for meaning in an unintelligible world – were in no way the fruit of that thirst for vengeance. I can state quite categorically that what I did and do is utterly removed from the logic of vengeance, not to excuse myself or lend a fraudulent moral veneer to my brief and modest experience in the field, but because I cannot remember ever being pleased to see another person's downfall or making the fight against tyranny a purely personal issue.

Viva the student movement!

In 2005 I arrived at university, burning with enthusiasm to participate in a great movement whose glories and heroism I had heard about since childhood: the student movement. A new chapter in my life was set to start, living out what I had dreamt of for so many years: I would give public speeches, lead marches, march in the footsteps of my glorious predecessors and lecture my contemporaries about the true meaning of freedom of speech and action.

I enrolled at the Preparatory Institute in Literary Studies and the Humanities, part of Tunis University, the same year that my brother Dhaffer graduated from the College of Economics and my sister Sana'a finished Year 9: a successful year for the family.

The fact was that my siblings and I had been determined to please my father, the engineering graduate barred from resuming his former profession, now the neighbourhood *épicier*, and bring a little joy to our mother who longed for us to do well at school. Our social standing was modest to say the least but we were armed with big dreams, convinced that the best was yet to come.

By the way, our names mean something. Dhaffer, the 'Victorious', was born in 1982 and my parents gave him his name because that was the year the Lebanese resistance was fighting off the Zionist invasion and required a victory to crush the enemy. Then, because my father knew there could be no victory without knowledge and proper planning he named me Malek after the great Algerian intellectual Malek Bennabi. I was born in 1985 and my sister in 1987, when she was named in honour of Sana'a Mehaidli, the resistance fighter who died on occupied Lebanese soil in the first ever female suicide bombing. While most people were naming their children after soap stars or because the names had a nice ring to them, my mother and father were naming us in solidarity with the pressing issues of the times, in particular the decades-long struggle over Palestine. This alone left a deep imprint on us.

So, I entered university in 2005. At that time I was, and perhaps still am, passionate about getting to know people: students from every corner of Tunisia, different cultures and dialects, different, and sometimes clashing, customs, ambitions and desires. I plunged into the scene wholeheartedly and, with nothing to hold me back, soon became a friend to all. I invited many people to the family home in Omrane supérieure and visited their rooms in the Avicenne Student Accommodation. The circle of my friends grew and I soon had a far-flung network of acquaintances that remains largely intact to this day.

The first weeks were a beautiful introduction to a world that was much as I had expected it: diverse and seductive. University meant absolute freedom, the destruction of the old and traditional and a passion for the new. It was there, in its lecture halls and classrooms, that I learned to criticize, to interrogate, to deconstruct, to philosophize and to ponder questions of existence, the universe and the human condition.

Gradually, my former feelings of vengeance against the regime transformed into a political consciousness. My desire to join the students' struggle against despotism intensified. I was full of life, burning with enthusiasm, 18 years old. I lived on the songs of Sheikh Imam, Marcel Khalife, an old Palestinian band called The Lovers and Bob Marley, the balladeers of commitment and revolution, but also Charles Aznavour, Edith Piaf and others with whom I travelled to other worlds of love and romance.

With good friends of mine from the Institute, I founded a negotiating committee for the General Union of Tunisian Students and we engaged in mighty confrontations against the regime and its educational policies. My early experiences in the union movement were some of the most wonderful of my life. I gained the love and respect of my peers, but this was not just an honour; it was a burden, too.

The start of the long road

The price was my expulsion from university.

In May 2007 the Institute convened an emergency disciplinary panel that voted to expel me and two of my comrades, Damir and Munji, on charges of 'defaming the president of the country, incitement against the regime, disseminating false information damaging to national security, distributing leaflets, inflaming citizens against the ruling party and seeking assistance from foreign elements'.

We turned the disciplinary hearing into an open-court trial against the Ministry of Higher Education and the regime itself, and the room where it was held into the cockpit of a struggle that exposed dictatorship.

I was an excellent student and the decision to expel me came as a genuine shock. I was unable to tell my family because I was afraid of how they would react, especially since I was being threatened with a blanket ban from all institutions of higher education, not to mention the possibility of being taken to court in view of 'the seriousness of the charges against me'.

It was days before I finally told the family what had happened and, as I had feared, the news hit them like a thunderbolt. Now all of us were wracked with nerves, fearful for my future.

On the other hand, when I was by myself I felt enormously happy and proud. My expulsion was like a membership card, an entry permit to the ranks of the struggle heroes. I was 19 now, and hoping to follow in the footsteps of my role models, particularly Mohamed Ali al-Hami (a Tunisian labour unionist and revolutionary of the 1920s), George

Habash (founder of the Popular Front for the Liberation of Palestine), Che Guevara, and all the martyrs of the Tunisian student movement: Fadil Sasi, Nabil Barakati and others. I believed, with a child's idealism and perhaps a touch of foolish arrogance, that fate had chosen me to continue with my father's and forefathers' struggle against dictatorship; that it was my duty to embrace my destiny, setting aside the world and its pleasures in pursuit of the noble cause for which I would sacrifice myself.

Big claims require big sacrifices.

The truth was that my expulsion was my first real test of my relationship with myself, my family, my comrades and my romanticized lifestyle. It was the moment I awoke from the intoxicated daze that had possessed me since the stormy start to my life as a student. Simply put, it was the moment of truth. I had grown up in a family that never interfered in my choices and I will never forget what my father said when he heard I had been sent down: 'I have complete faith in what you do, so you must have faith in what you do.'

It brought my feet back to earth after I had been soaring in the clouds with my eyes tight shut. I realized that the world of unions and politics had many faces and not all of those who moved in it were the honest and honourable freedom lovers I had imagined them to be, but included the unstable, the opportunists, the brokers, the cheats and the liars as well. All this I discovered gradually, over the course of many battles, and as much as it shocked me to have my rosy stereotype of the 'noble comrade' shaken so severely, it also left me wiser and calmer. I started listening to what wasn't being said, reading between the lines and prising out what lay behind the ringing phrases.

I spent the summer of 2007 at sit-ins by the Ministry of Higher Education, the Presidency of Tunis University, the Preparatory Institute and the colleges of the humanities, protesting against our expulsion and asking union-affiliated professors to intervene on behalf of myself and my two comrades. I was acting alone, without any political or media support, even from those comrades supposedly closest to me. I felt I had been abandoned; that I was somehow expendable in the fight for some greater cause. At the time, I vowed that I would continue the struggle my own way: I would leave no stone unturned to expose any union or political activities that betrayed the ethics and traditions of the student movement.

I was successful. In October, 2008, myself, Damir and Munji, enrolled at the April 9 Faculty of Human and Social Sciences, the great academic institution that helped found modern Tunisia and the first university institution to be founded after independence in 1956, with its politically conscious students and academic rigour. This is what attracted me in the first instance: it was one of the strongholds of the struggle. We called it 'the Vietnam of Tunis University'. It was famous for its public plaza, Red Square, a wide, rectangular expanse of tarmac enclosed by four huge walls, where the major student demonstrations were held, with activists and revolutionaries flocking from all parts of the country to organize mass strikes and boisterous public meetings.

Walking into the April 9 college was a watershed moment in my life. I spent a total of four years there, learning what could not be learnt anywhere else. April 9 is lived, not told; April 9 welcomes you into its awe-inspiring, high-walled square and infuses you with culture and scholarship. But its spirit is what makes it as it is. It is the cries of the massed students, the speeches of union activists, and the manifestos of marginalized politics.

At April 9 I debated and discussed; I warred and skirmished, if I may be excused my self-aggrandizing words. I entered a fiercely partisan Marxist and left a dogmatic atheist. I entered a believer in laws and determinism and left a believer in plurality and knowledge. I was at the forefront of strikes and protests that disturbed the sleep of tyrants. I wrote hundreds of articles and texts, proselytizing, analyzing and criticizing. I remember my first intervention, when I called on people to remember their dignity, 'in the name of those who raise the hoes and shovels, in the name of those who make scythes from swords', I became an ambassador for April 9 at the other colleges, starting fronts, drawing up movements, overseeing demonstrations, creating unionists and founding branches for the General Student Union. When I look at myself in the mirror now, I see April 9 written there and I see, etched in my face, expressions of anger, joy, anticipation, pain and ecstasy: all the feelings that swept over me then.

I also owe April 9 and Red Square a debt of gratitude for introducing me to Ezza Darbali. I'm not sure if this is the place to talk about it, not because it's a private matter but because there is so much to say and I always surprise myself how loquacious I can be when the subject comes up. Memories overwhelm me: the first shoots of love, feelings aflame, the first flirtatious glances. The pen turns it all to poetry.

17 December 2010

I was in the college library when a friend from Sidi Bouzid phoned to let me know that a young man from the city had immolated himself inside the governor's headquarters in protest against the beating and humiliation he had suffered at the hands of the municipal police. Hundreds of enraged citizens were gathered outside the building in an open sit-in, demanding to be told the truth and paying their respects to the victim.

The news was shocking and painful. Such suicides had been taking place regularly in Tunisia (the most recent had been that of Abdel Salam Trimsh in Monastir on 11 March 2010), the product of poverty, unemployment and a sense of degradation and indignity that reflected the frustration and despair felt by young men throughout Tunisia.

All Saturday long I kept in contact with a friend of mine, a participant in the sit-in and an eyewitness, who kept me up to speed with the latest developments. From him, I learnt that it was turning into a protest against the local authorities, then that a mass protest movement was taking shape, as more and more angry citizens poured into the street.

When Mohamed Bouazizi set fire to his body it was the drop that made the cup run over: the sit-in mutated into vast marches decrying corruption and marginalization and demanding jobs and dignity. The city of Sidi Bouzid did not sleep that night. In various neighbourhoods and alleyways clashes broke out between angry young protestors and the police, who increased their presence on the main roads into the city.

Things were moving on apace and we in the capital tried to keep abreast of developments, which included creating effective forms of support for the protestors, trying to break the blackout imposed by the State media and making people feel the justice of the protestors' demands.

The student movement and the people

On the morning of Sunday, 19 December, I came to a cafe in a suburb of Tunis to meet some comrades from the General Union of Tunisian Students. We decided to launch a series of general strikes in all the colleges to demand an immediate halt to the brutal repression of the protestors and to insist that their demands be taken seriously. The challenge was how to ensure the strikes succeeded, since the students were about to stop taking classes and begin revising for their exams. This meant that the colleges were almost empty, and only a few students were willing to engage in confrontations at such a crucial juncture in the academic year.

We spent the Sunday looking over our options until we had agreed on a provisional working plan. With some of my Facebook contacts I arranged to set up a page called

The Tunisian Street Protest News Agency and issue a digital bulletin in Arabic, French and English, which first saw the light on 26 December, under the name 'The Resistance Diaries'.

We felt it was necessary to inform, mobilize and counter State propaganda all at the same time so the protestors in Sidi Bouzid would not find themselves alone and vulnerable as happened in 2008 in the revolt at the Gafsa mining basin, where protests lasted six months before the authorities were able to quash them and imprison the leaders.

Students returned to the April 9 college on Monday, 3 January 2011, following the end of the half-term break, and we witnessed a gradual escalation. Posters were hung on walls, pamphlets handed out; discussion circles and open meetings were our daily bread. Unrest spread through Sidi Bouzid, to Meknassy, Menzel Bouzaiane and Regueb in the first phase, then Mezzouna, Sidi Ali Ben Aoun and Jilma in the second. The geographical limits of the protests fanned out and their slogans became blunter.

In the college we became more confrontational. The blind, brutal repression of the movement let rage and disgust grow. On a number of occasions we clashed with police who had besieged the college and blocked off the entrances, trying to get out and join the student marches denouncing repression and demanding dignity. Although the exams were about to start, the college witnessed mass rallies the like of which had not been seen for years, most of them ending in bloody battles with policemen wielding clubs and firing tear gas.

April 9 was one of the few citadels that had held out against dictatorship over the years, supplying the political opposition with fresh cadres. It is a large college, of about 8,000 students, but kept its secrets hidden from outside eyes behind tall walls and the beautiful marble reliefs on its main entrance. Walking through the students' entrance you find yourself before 'the little square' that usually plays host to union meetings. Facing you on the other side of the square stands an unattached building housing the six lecture halls. To its left is a vast wall: the outer wall of the college. You enter the noisy student cafeteria from the little square and exit into one of Tunisia's most famous sites of learning and political resistance: Red Square. In the middle of the square sits 'the star', a circular depression one and a half metres deep, once a fountain, where various student factions meet to debate and discuss. The edge of the square, nearest the student cafe, is where the large student rallies took place.

To complement the struggle inside the college grounds we had our own 'Freedom Square': Mohamed Ali Square, opposite the headquarters of the Tunisian Labour Union; a large square metres away from Avenue Habib Bourguiba and long a refuge for unionists defending their rights and other freedoms, in part because the Labour Union (UGTT), which rivals the ruling party in terms of membership and clout, is such a powerful supporter of the struggle.

In this square we took part in workers' rallies organized by the major unions in support of our countrymen in Sidi Bouzid. Most of the time we were attending these rallies in our private capacities, outside the organizational structures of the Student Union. We would try and turn them into marches along Avenue Habib Bourguiba but the police and rapid response units reacted violently to any attempt to break through their lines and leave the square. I swear to you, I experienced moments of epic heroism by students, union members and female activists as they confronted the clubs and sticks of the thuggish police.

For many days we divided our time between the university and Mohamed Ali Square, challenging the official line that portrayed the protestors in Sidi Bouzid as 'masked bandits' who wished Tunisia ill and were carrying out a 'destructive' agenda. The regime would 'punish them' as Ben Ali had stated in December.

In the eyes of my fellow citizens I saw an extraordinary determination to confront the forces of repression. I got the feeling that I was witnessing a movement that – as no other before – would shake the regime to its foundations. The protestors' eyes gleamed with resolve and courage, their raised palms and V-signs waved tirelessly and their throats bellowed out the slogans of freedom and dignity.

At night myself and other comrades would daub walls with the slogans of the protest movement:

Al-tashghil istihqaq, ya 'isaba al-siraq! Employment's a right, you gang of thieves!
Ya shahid, irtah irtah! Sanuwassil al-kifah! Sleep easy, martyr, we will continue the fight!
Ya muwatin! Ya dahiya! Ta' sharik fil-qadiya! Citizen! Victim! Join the cause!

I remember being chased by a National Guard vehicle that had surprised us as we were about to write on the walls of the secondary school in Omrane supérieure. We managed to escape through the backstreets, chanting 'Guardians of the Guardian!' and shouting for the downfall of the regime.

On Facebook we published our electronic edition of 'The Resistance Diaries'. In three languages it told the world the truth of what was happening in Tunisia. In the first edition I wrote an article entitled, 'A week in the fight against the rolling machinery of repression'. The bulletin's production team consisted of no more than ten young men and women, every one a student, and I remember them all: Sana'a, Iman, Mohamed Ali, Ziad, Ghassan, Tariq, Leila, Jihad, Nabil, and my sweetheart, Ezza.

We worked in a wonderfully sharing atmosphere and the way we complemented each other was truly incredible. This bulletin was our link to journalists, activists and revolutionaries in Tunisia and overseas. The first edition was an act of citizenship, issued during the protests in order to create an alternative media, which presented events from the perspective of the Tunisian public, opposing despotism. Our work on the bulletin later branched out into many other projects, the most prominent of which was the Tunisian Street Protest News Agency page on Facebook, which gained a wide following for its honesty and accuracy, followed by We are all Mohamed Bouazizi and other coordinating groups on the site whose access was restricted to the activist leadership.

Besieging the siege: no escape

At the beginning of January something important happened: the protests spread to the governorate of Kasserine. After 15 days of resistance in Sidi Bouzid and its surroundings, neighbouring Kasserine caught fire, with my city of Tala at the cutting edge of events. Residents rose up against the social misery that weighed the city down and were immediately confronted with the terror of brutal and relentless security forces.

Of course, the dire conditions that led the inhabitants of Sidi Bouzid to protest and demonstrate were a part of reality that extended through other parts of the country, and nowhere more so than in the governorate of Kasserine.

This development transformed me, for the simple reason that my roots lay in this anonymous, impoverished city. When the protests were confined to Sidi Bouzid I had given my all in the fight against corruption and despotism, but as they spread to Tala, where my relatives lived, where I was raised and lived the happiest days of my life, a peculiar feeling came over me.

I have never been the slightest bit tribal or sectarian or viewed things through the lens of personal interest or partisan concern for my family or region. From the moment I entered university in 2005 I had been a member of the student movement, wholly concerned with the marginalized and forgotten. Yet when I saw the first images of armoured vehicles rolling into the main street in Tala and heard reports of the torture and rape taking place in the city, my feelings boiled over. I lost all self-control: the ability to think rationally and assess the consequences of my actions.

One of the most tragic moments came on the evening of 8 January.

Unaware that the first martyrs had fallen in Tala, among them close friends such as Marwan Jumali, Ghassan Sheniti and others, I came home to find my mother and her brother Abdel Jabbar in the house. My uncle was weeping bitterly and my mother was beside herself. Both of them were tough characters. So many disasters had befallen them in the past and they had always held firm so something extraordinary must have happened. I assumed a member of the family must have been martyred: maybe my cousin Mohamed, or cousin Kamal. My cousins were on the front lines of the battle for the city and it was through them that I was closely following the protests.

There was a dreadful silence in the house, broken only by tortured sobs and groans. I didn't ask them what had happened. I didn't need to. I went outside, not knowing what to do. My mother caught up with me, trying to persuade me not to leave for fear of what I might do. I convinced her that I needed fresh air.

That is when I made up my mind to go to Tala, persuading myself that my presence there, alongside the young men of the city, was more important than remaining in the college that was already ablaze with rage and protests. The fact is, I was incapable of thinking rationally. I was in the grip of an unreasoning passion to participate in the resistance on the ground. I told no one of my decision except two or three friends, whom I swore to silence on the pretext of security.

I knew that reaching Tala the usual way by taxi or bus would be impossible because the police controlled the entrances to the city and were checking ID cards, but my main difficulty was not getting there so much as finding brave companions to make the journey with me. I called my cousin Ziad, who worked as a truck driver transporting marble from Tala to Tunis. We met in a suburb of the capital and I made my offer. He accepted without hesitation. He was on edge and angry at what had happened.

At approximately 11 in the evening on 8 January we set out for Kef, 70 kilometres north of Tala. I was carrying no identity papers, had shaved off my hair and beard and was wrapped in a *qashabiya*, a kind of winter cloak they wear in Tala. To my mother I wrote a short letter that I left with a friend from our neighbourhood. I did not think I would ever return to Tunis.

We reached Kef at two in the morning. We had only passed through a single checkpoint coming into town and they had checked the truck's documents without bothering about our identities. The road to Tala began at a crossroads where highways led off in all directions: Tala, Downtown Kef, Dahmani and Tunis. Unwilling to risk taking the conventional and quickest way, which would mean passing through a series of police, army and National Guard checkpoints, we took the scenic route through Dahmani and El Ksour, then on to the bumpy country roads by Jedelienne and Aiaoun. It was a long and arduous journey, but at 4:30 that morning we entered the countryside around Tala from the direction of Jebel Boulhenache.

We stopped the truck to rest for a while. Said, a friend from Tala, insisted we stay where we were and not gamble on making it into the city, but we wanted to reach one of the surrounding hills. Tala is built on a rocky outcrop with hills on every side. From our position we could see the city in the distance, dim lights glowing in the darkness, and, straining our ears could make out the staccato patter of gunfire. I will never forget those moments. It was like a scene from a film, a fragment of a dream.

My friend and I decided to approach the city on foot before the sun rose. Leaving the truck we set out, our senses alive.

For almost an hour we walked along a back lane, urging ourselves onwards. Suddenly, a volley of gunfire burst out, deafening us. We could see the glow of the bullets as they rained against the facade of houses in Najariya in West Tala. We had to hurry. Dawn was almost upon us.

We continued our labyrinthine run into the city. Friends inside Tala had told us we could make it in via the marble quarries and so we did. Just as the sun came up we entered Tala through a rubbish dump outside Najariya, a route I cannot bring myself to describe to this day. Whenever I remember it or try to talk about it a shudder runs through me. But it was on that journey, for a few brief moments, that I lost the fear, the terror even, which had been my constant companion since we set out on foot.

Tala: the Stalingrad of North Africa

I was not exhausted: I was on fire. Surrounded by these anonymous young men, eager to defend their city and determined to take revenge on the 'enemy' who had murdered the best of them in cold blood, it felt as though I was in the midst of patriotic resistance fighters, baring their breasts to the forces of some merciless foreign foe.

In the clashes that took place on the night of 8 January, seven martyrs fell. The young protestors had barely managed to drag their bodies from the battlefield in the city centre. With my own eyes I saw the corpses smiling in death and mothers ululating through the rain of bullets and the horror, weeping over the bodies of their beloved children.

Dark-skinned, palms torn by the rocks they had hurled, legs bloodied by constant running and falling, the young men wrapped the martyrs' brows in linen and vowed, by the honour of the city and the bread and poverty they had shared, to continue the fight and kill their killers.

From the early morning cries of 'God is great', ululations and wails rose into the air. The coming hours would decide the outcome of the battle. The security forces and the decision makers back in Tunis knew that after these acts of murder the city would be transformed into a district of hell itself. The men and women of the city and their sons and daughters knew that to back down now meant death and imprisonment for each and every one of them.

Three funeral processions set out from Najariya. I joined one at the southern entrance to the neighbourhood. The corpses were laid on wool blankets, there for all to see: their bodies, clothes and blood untouched. I helped carry the casket of one of the martyrs. We chanted as we went:

Ya shahid irtah irtah, sanuwassil al-kifah! Sleep easy, martyr, we will continue the fight!
Al-shahid khali wasiya, la tnazil 'al-qadiya! The martyr has left his will: never abandon the cause!
Ya Marwan ya shahid! 'ala darbak la nahid! Marwan, our martyr! We will never stray from your path!

People flocked to the processions in epic scenes reminiscent of Palestine: men and women, old men and children, weeping, wailing, ululating, popular anthems and traditional songs, wild dancing and screams.

All Tala came out to bid its sons farewell. We were joined by residents of every neighbourhood in the city, people of all backgrounds. The funeral cortèges came together and a roaring human wave set out for the city's cemetery. It was at that moment that the police, stationed by the southern entrance, opened fire on the mourners with tear gas and a hail of bullets.

We laid the bodies on the ground for which they had given their lives and the people turned to confront the machine. It was a genuine street battle and it claimed another martyr from amongst the mourners. The young men were determined to bury their martyrs and they paid the price. We resumed our march to the cemetery with the stench of gas and smoke filling the air.

Everyone was there. The sight of them digging and pre-paring the graves made my heart bleed. They scrabbled with their fingernails, tears wetting their cheeks. The mourners raised a cry, and as I chanted with them I was convinced that the Palace of Carthage and all who dwelt within it would be razed to the ground. Bitter and angry, alive and courageous, thousands shouted as one:

Ya al-Zine, sabrak sabrak! Fi Tala nahfir qabrak!
Ben Ali, have patience! We're digging your grave in Tala!

We would dig the President's grave here in Tala. We would have our revenge for our sons and brothers.

This terrible cry was the starkest challenge yet uttered, for it referred to the President by name and threatened him not just with deposition or exile, but with death and the vengeance of the inhabitants of this isolated region. It was a hugely symbolic moment.

The burial service lasted nearly two hours and ended with resumed hostilities. Each side took up their position: the police in the main road and the protestors in the backstreets and alleys. My relatives had no idea I was here. I preferred to remain alongside the 'warriors'. I was no good at making Molotov cocktails and useless with a slingshot, so I would throw rocks during street battles and draw up plans to lure the police into the alleys and passages where we were strongest.

By the evening I was famished and utterly exhausted. I slipped away from Ziad the truck driver and went looking for an out of the way spot to get some rest. I was in a wretched state, torn apart by conflicting emotions: anger and contentment, pain and joy. With the young protestors of Tala I had wanted to pursue the possibility of centralizing a 'field command' for the protests: a framing committee, an organizing committee, a continuity committee – something along those lines. My union background made me argue for at least some degree of organization, but I gradually came to realize that the secret to our success was partly down to our chaotic state, or rather, the number and variety of leaders and the absence of a domineering centralized command that would stifle initiative and hinder immediate responses to a rapidly developing situation on the ground.

I ate an egg (how I got hold of an egg, I have no idea) with a hot loaf of the local bread called *tabouna* and drank gallons of water: the revolutionary meal. Then we set out again to the front lines at Najariya, which were somewhat calmer now. I later discovered that many of the security forces assigned to Tala had gone to the city of Kasserine.

I was with two young men, neither of them older than 20. They were delighted that I was here: a student from the capital returned to defend his birthplace. There were some differences in the dialect and the maze of alleys in Najariya was a mystery to me, but here I was. From my brief conversation with the pair of them I gained an idea of just how poorly treated this city had been. Neither had any conception of the State beyond the police, the criminal courts, tear gas and live rounds. The regime treated them as enemies. And why? they asked. Why are we different to the young people of the coastal cities? Their question struck at the heart of Tunisia's political system and the development model that had been adopted since independence: one of colonial exploitation.

That night the clashes continued here and there. I managed to locate Ziad, or rather, he managed to locate me. I was tired and worried about my mother, who would be wondering where I was. Our discussion revolved around relieving the pressure on Tala, Kasserine and Sidi Bouzid. We talked about the important role played by unionists and lawyers but the solution, we decided, was starting protests in working-class districts in the major cities, especially in Tunis. This would break the back of the regime.

Back to Tunis

I felt I needed to return to the capital, where I might be more useful. Deep down I believed that the popular movement in Tunis would decide the battle. Not because it was the capital city and the centre of the country, but because it could not be cut off and isolated like the provinces, something confirmed by the history of popular uprisings in Tunisia.

The journey back was if anything even harder. Just getting out of Najariya and finding the truck took hours. Luckily Ziad knew the country roads like the back of his hand. With the problem of transport sorted and my goodbyes said, I sat in the truck reviewing the events of the past day. It was as though a week had gone by: so many unforgettable incidents and sights, so many emotions. I surrendered to sleep and was woken by my relative when we reached the Majaz al-Bab–Tunis highway, so I could take over at the wheel and give him a break.

We reached Tunis at 10 o'clock on Monday morning and parted company outside the bus stop in Bab Alioua. There were two choices before me: go home, or go to the college. It was only then that I turned on my mobile phone, which I had switched off the moment we entered Tala: text messages and voicemails from my family, friends from college and my girlfriend Ezza. I decided to head for the college and go home later.

I went to Bab al-Jazira Street, then to Bab al-Manara, and in the Kasbah two vehicles that I recognized as belonging to the political police caught my attention. During major student demonstrations at the college the political police would detain influential unionists and release them in the evening to ensure things did not get out of hand. For a moment I thought that I was going to be detained and I sent a text message to Abdel Rahman, a fellow student union activist at the college letting him know I was in Government Square in the Kasbah and in danger of being kidnapped, and he should spread the word if I didn't arrive in the next ten minutes.

Right outside the Museum of Cinema I saw the white Renault Clio come speeding up against the traffic and I was sure I must be the target. The street was almost empty and I had neither the time nor energy to make a run for it, so I stayed where I was on the pavement. The car pulled up next to me and four men got out, one of whom I recognized as part of a team who came to the college to observe unionists and political activists. The men asked me not to put up a struggle and get quietly into the car.

I didn't budge. I looked left and right down the street in a desperate attempt to find a way out but it was too late: one of them handcuffed me and they forced me onto the back seat. In no time they were all back in the car with me and we set off. Removing my handcuffs they politely informed me that they were under orders and had nothing personal against me.

We drove by the college and I craned my head round to see my comrades busy with a public meeting and preparing to head out on a march. All around the college sat riot control units while inside it seethed with students. I smiled and politely asked the men to tell me why I had been stopped and where they were taking me.

Nobody answered. Having just returned from Tala the prospect of interrogation and detention frightened me. The thought popped into my head that I would be tried for participating in civil disorder, attacking security forces, defaming the President and similar charges. Had they found out that I had only just come back from Tala? Was there anything at all the government didn't know? Simultaneously, I was trying to figure out where we were going by keeping my eye on the road. We were on April 9 Street heading for the coastal road. What security facility could it be? Which police station? It wasn't at all clear to me and I pictured them driving me out to the Mohamediya Road outside Tunis as they had done to me before, back in 2009.

After a few minutes it became clear that their orders had come through. I heard the driver say, 'Got it; understood,' into his mobile. He changed direction and they put a hood over my head so I couldn't tell where we were going.

About half an hour later I sensed that the car had stopped and heard the engine switching off. The four of them got out and one of them removed the hood. I climbed out. I had no idea where I was. A road surrounded by trees and bushes. As I peered about one of them ordered me to lie on the ground. I looked at him and the four of them began hitting me until I fell down then continued to hit me as I lay there. One of them opened my mobile and flung it away then they got back in the car and drove off.

I pulled myself together and after a long search managed to retrieve the phone. I called my friends and told them what had happened.

I had been driven to the Jebel Amar Road off the highway to Bizerte, beaten up and dumped. These were their orders. I sat in the middle of the road and roared with laughter at the sheer oddness of what I'd been through. How surreal! What kind of government treats its opposition like that?

I called a neighbour who turned up a couple of hours later to take me home. Despite my mother demanding to know where I had spent the previous night I fell asleep and slept for a long time.

On the morning of 11 January I learnt that the government had closed all educational establishments after the colleges and secondary schools had been transformed into centres of protest. We had lost the engine room of our movement. Exams were suspended, the school gates were locked and Mohamed Ali Square had become our final refuge.

Death for us, terror for them

At three in the afternoon I met up with a group of friends and we held long discussions about how we would proceed now the university had been closed down. As in Tala, we reached the conclusion that the battle must move into the working-class districts.

At 6 o'clock I was with a union activist called Nabil, sitting in a cafe in the Tahrir neighbourhood. Ramzi was in Tadamon, the biggest working-class neighbourhood in the city, and when I called him he told me clashes had broken out with the police in Area 105. We immediately set out to see for ourselves.

We reached Intilaqa, in the suburbs of Tunis, by the entrance to Tadamon where we were joined by Bairam, a union activist from April 9 college, and witnessed the security forces preparing to move into the neighbourhood. I phoned Ramzi again and learnt that there was a tense stand-off in Area 105 and it looked very probable that the police would mount another assault. I knew the area well and crossing the security cordon we headed over to where groups of young men stood about, keeping an eye on the situation and ready to respond if the security forces entered the neighbourhood. The police addressed us through a loudspeaker, asking us to vacate the area and when the youths showed no sign of obeying orders the police began firing tear gas. Some of the canisters dropped at our feet while others fell on rooftops, an unprovoked tactic that enraged the local residents.

Then the clashes started. The battlefield was a maze of narrow alleyways and the police suffered heavy losses, surrounded on four sides and bombarded with rocks. Taken by surprise they retreated and we repaired first to the local headquarters of the ruling party, which we regarded as nests of traitors, in order to occupy them and purge them, and then to the police stations. Various battles broke out which ended in victory for the protestors. It was a war between unemployed, frustrated and angry youths who saw the chance to vent their suffering and a police force utterly ignorant of the topography of the battlefield and their opponents' psychology.

My comrades and I were determined to start political chants calling for the downfall of the regime, like, 'Down with the Constitutional Party! Down with the executioners of the people!' and 'Down with the November 7 Regime: repressive, traitorous, sell-outs!'

This would help them give expression to their anger. We were at the front of the crowds, urging them to resist, because we knew that the tyrant's throne was shaking and victory was at hand.

Once the neighbourhood had been completely 'liberated' of its police presence we got news of clashes taking place in neighbourhoods like Karam, Sidi Hassine and Kabariya and we left. I preferred to stay away from my home because I believed the authorities were sure to carry out a series of mass detentions. We went to the city centre to spend the night following developments from there.

We had been sitting at a cafe in Bab al-Khadra for about half an hour when we were joined by three more friends who lived nearby. There were now six of us in total and we decided to move on after we grew suspicious that the cafe's patrons included informers for internal security. Almost the instant we left the cafe we were picked up by a patrol.

It was like talking to a brick wall. We told them we were unionists, members of UGET (the General Union of Tunisian Students), while they swore at us and abused the organization. They were clearly tense and one of their number, their resident genius, noticed the Palestinian *kuffayah* I wore over my shoulders and decided that we must be opponents of the regime, one of the 'masked bandits' Ben Ali had spoken of.

The balance of power was not in our favour. We didn't put up a struggle. We were taken to the Nahj Cologna police station. I had always believed that when one of us was detained it was part of a carefully weighed political strategy, not the spontaneous initiative of individual policemen. But the moment I walked into the station this time, I felt that the authorities were moving in the direction of fire and steel and the new 'orders' from above would pay scant regard to the old niceties.

The policemen searched us thoroughly, taking away our mobile phones, handcuffing us then lining us up against the wall. We stayed like that for about half an hour, waiting for the station command to arrive, but in his place we got the head of the political police for Bab al-Bahr, the man responsible for political investigations in central Tunis. He knew us all well. His squad had been responsible for operations against countless student protests, not to mention beating, detaining and conducting surveillance against activists and revolutionaries. He had personally overseen the torture, fabrication of charges and imprisonment of many of our comrades. And we knew him, too. We considered him one of the biggest 'torturers' of them all, who thanks to his contacts among senior figures in the Ministry of Interior, enjoyed carte blanche to act as he pleased.

He was not surprised to see us. He congratulated the policemen on capturing such a 'fat prize' and walked along the line examining our faces. Gloating and arrogant he pulled a knife from the folds of his overcoat and waved it in front of us. He paused when he got to me and peered into my eyes. I frowned and did not drop my head as he had anticipated but stared back at him with the same cold gaze. He began to seethe and a brief, silent conversation passed between us, from which I understood that this man meant to make an example of us.

After two hours of psychological torture and continuous threats we were taken to the National Security Compound in Bab al-Bahr in the company of the political police chief. During the short trip over I spotted a tank parked in Passage Square, a large public space in central Tunis opposite the Public Gardens. It was the first time the army had entered the capital. I whispered in the ear of one of my companions on the back seat that things were coming to a head and that our fate was in the hands of the victor: either the people or the dictatorship. If the people were triumphant then we would be heroes, but if the dictatorship won out we would be among the first to lose our lives.

The moment we arrived we were met by members of the Crime Fighting Unit and roughly handled. Cuffed, we sat on cold metal chairs linked in a line: six of us to four chairs and we stayed like that for nearly two hours until we were led off for individual interrogation. I had thought that we would be brought to trial on trumped-up charges as a lesson to other protestors and the only thing that bothered me was the thought of my family and how they would cope with the idea that I was a prisoner.

At times such as these the mind remains perfectly clear, capable of thinking calmly in the face of all one's fear of the unknown. I did not lose my cool in front of the policeman who tried to extract a confession from me that I had burnt and destroyed police stations and ruling party buildings, that I had distributed inflammatory material and made speeches calling for the downfall of the regime.

My companions and I went through some very personal experiences. Knowing that they were determined to frame us we became linked by a unique bond: more than mere friendship or companionship, it was a profound kind of solidarity that perhaps stemmed from the fact we were facing a common fate out of love for our country and that we were ready to sacrifice ourselves for its sake. And now, the time for sacrifice had come: the test of the principles and values for which we had fought. We would steal glances at one another and smile, charging ourselves with the positive energy of resolve, determination and courage.

At nine in the morning they led us out again, shackled hand and foot. This time, I thought, we are going to the Bouchoucha detention centre, but when we had climbed into the police car the head of internal security turned his head and told us: 'You are going to be punished most severely. Most severely. See you later.'

It was a line taken word for word from Ben Ali's second speech, which he addressed directly to the 'masked bandits'.

Ten minutes later we were in the Interior Ministry, that

mysterious, sinister, imposing building that squats in the middle of Avenue Habib Bourguiba, receiving blows to every part of our bodies.

The Ministry of Interior

From the very first moment, even as we were being searched and our personal effects confiscated (phones, cash, papers), we were being punched and kicked. We were lined up along a wall, cuffed and shackled, forbidden to move or speak or lift our heads. I remember thinking at the time that I had experienced this before, in Abdelrahman Munif's novel *Sharq al-Mutawassit*, perhaps, or stories about the Burj al-Rumi prison (a notorious prison in the coastal town of Bizerte). It was the experience of prison literature, the literature of human tragedy, where the prison guard stands before you exposed as human beast, where the pain is more than language can capture, where everything takes place far from eyes and ears, inside caves or darkened dungeons that belong to a world of unfettered savagery.

They took us down to a cell, photographed us and sat us on chairs facing the wall. I don't know how long we stayed like that. From that point onwards I lost the ability to estimate time, in fact, from that point onwards we stepped outside time altogether; lost our link to the passage of night and day.

In that terrifying place we were metres below Avenue Habib Bourguiba, the biggest, most important thoroughfare in the capital, pulsing with life, a tourist promenade with sparkling street lights, its cafes packed with patrons, ringing with the laughter of passers-by, its restaurants and shops always full. Over our heads lay the land of the living in its most splendid incarnation, while down below we sat in the land of the dead. Such violent contrast, separated by scant metres; a contradiction to drive one mad.

Out of the corner of my eye I could see part of the cell, like a large warehouse or public square: gleaming white cement tiles and a high ceiling hung with spotlights that seared the eyes. There were eight doors, as far as I could tell, each one concealing its secrets behind blue frames. The voices of Interior Ministry agents sounded anonymously. We could hear them but not see them as they beat us for whatever reason, or for none.

Alongside us were the corpses of two individuals draped in a filthy covering. It was obvious they had been subjected to terrible torture. They were nearly naked and I could make out their feet and legs coated in blood. This sight was extremely disturbing and I pictured myself in their place, though I quickly realized that this was part of their plan to terrify us. Even so, weren't these two human corpses? Did they slowly murder people just to frighten others?

My companions and I were utterly exhausted but, despite the long wait that was quite enough by itself to destroy anyone's resolve, we remained alert. On more than one occasion we silently conversed with each other out of the corners of our eyes, because hands would rain down if one of us so much as turned his head. We were encouraging one another, boosting our morale and hoping that things would turn out well, though deep down we knew that this was just the calm before the storm.

'Gordon' came in. That's what they called him. A hoarse voice welcomed him and the heavy tread of footsteps told us that the two men were approaching us. Gordon began to beat us all in turn: everyone got a fair portion of this human animal's feast. He slapped me viciously over my right ear and I felt great pain and an irritating ringing in my head. The hoarse voice informed him that I was 'their leader' and that I was 'dangerous and an irritant' so he bit my neck and throttled me with both hands until I could not breathe. Since I was comprehensively restrained I was unable to defend myself, so I just shut my eyes, stiffened and moaned.

Two men grabbed one of us and took him off somewhere. I heard the sound of the metal door through which we had entered the cell open, then close. It was a huge door in the left-hand corner. I had no idea what they would do to him, but some kind of answer was provided by the broken sobs that issued now and then from the surrounding rooms and the two corpses lying next to me. They were giving us a lesson in man's ability to carry out acts of savagery.

At regular intervals, every hour or so, they would pick one of us up and disappear with him behind the door. I was the last one to leave the cell: utterly exhausted, hungry and troubled by the questions that kept leaping into my head. They put something like a blindfold over my eyes and I walked up a long staircase, three or four floors in total, then down a short hallway and into a small room.

They removed the blindfold and left my shackles on. Two men in their thirties came in, they locked the door and sat down before me and the interrogation began. They asked me about everything, about things that had nothing to do with my union or political activities, about my friends, family and neighbours. I told them what I believed they must already know.

No one hit me and after two hours they led me back down to the cell. None of my friends were there and they put me in Room 6. I threw myself down and slept. How long I slept I don't know, all that matters is that I woke to the squeaking of the door to see the guards throw two more young men into the room before dragging me roughly away. They replaced the handcuffs, whose removal I had not enjoyed at all, threw a hood over my head and took me upstairs.

This time, though, there was only one investigator, an old man with sparks flying from his eyes. This was a political interrogation. He questioned me about my intellectual and political connections and affiliations, my activism, my beliefs, my writings and my speeches. Everything was looked into.

He peered hard at me, walking around and around the cold metal chair on which I sat. Gently resting his hand on my shoulder he whispered in my ear: 'I'm your only friend in here. If you're not honest with me then I can't defend you to my colleagues, and they're waiting to rip you apart.'

I knew this was an interrogation technique and deep down I was convinced, though I don't know why, that he was even worse than his colleagues. Even so, I took advantage of the situation to ask him for a cigarette. I hadn't smoked for days. Rather reluctantly he lit me one and handed it over. I took a deep drag and blew out, expelling all the fear and worry that had accumulated in my chest with the smoke.

A few moments passed then he sat down in front of me and opened a red file full of papers. It appeared to be my personal file, the one that contained every word and whisper that had passed my lips since my mother brought me into the world. He opened his mouth and began: 'In 1991, inside this building but in a different room, I was one of those who interrogated your father.'

He said this with no emotion, looking at me and leafing through the documents in the file. I had to pick my words very carefully, with just seconds, sometimes only fractions of a second, to weigh my response to a question or provocation. I must not appear confused or evasive or dishonest (though I admit I became quite a good liar during this period).

'I hope God grants you a long life that you might get to interrogate my son as well.'

My answer took him by surprise. Lifting his head, he frowned and fixed me with an angry glare. He hadn't expected me to say what I did and, truth be told, nor had I. Nevertheless, I enjoyed it. I was about to embark on a war of words with one of the high priests of State security and I was treating it much like a formal debate, where both sides draw on all their reserves of eloquence and persuasiveness to see their thesis triumph. The only difference, of course, was that my opponent was also the adjudicator. It was a challenge. For a brief instant

I escaped the bounds of time and place, the weight of this reality, and stared back into the eyes of the 'expert' who sat across from me.

I was an official in the General Union of Tunisian Students, I told him. I was bound by the decisions and structures of my organization and had no affiliation with any other party or group. The views I expressed were likewise a function of my duty to the union.

When he despaired of extracting a confession from me he lost his temper and left the room. Two other men came in with no other task than to beat me up.

I took a savage beating that day, curling up in a ball to protect my face and moaning in pain as they tried to break my will with force alone.

I have never been beaten with such ferocity, nor have I seen it happen to anyone else. For a few moments I floated outside myself and watched it happen. It was as though I had been split in two: one half observing the body twisting beneath the blows. The pain was so severe I could no longer feel it: only a great tiredness and a desire to vomit and scream.

It is hard to talk or write about the experience of torture. The tongue and fingers tremble and hesitate, not out of a desire to forget, but rather to protect the memory. I am frightened that I might forget even the smallest detail of what I felt then. Anger, sadness, pain and joy, experienced in the selfsame instant: a sensation that lies beyond the power of metaphor.

It stayed like this for some time and, I believe, for my friends as well. They would drag me off for interrogation. Twice a day, I think. They would provide one vile meal bracketed by two sessions of questioning and beating.

One night they didn't take me to the usual cell but to a more spacious room on the top floor. They undressed me and I was subjected to a bestial hysteria. I remember one of the torturers opening the window to let me hear what he described as the people chanting for Ben Ali (I later found out this was 13 January, when the President made a speech promising reforms). I could hear car horns but I couldn't make out what people were saying. I was fearfully dizzy and the blood, sweat and lack of sleep prevented me from understanding what was going on.

That night was truly hellish. For a time I believed that they were certainly intending to kill me and my mind was full of all the Islamists who had been tortured to death in this very building during the 1990s. Yet some voice inside me told me that the people would be victorious.

Exhaustion had taken a heavy toll and a constant stream of blood and pus leaked from my ear. Their approach had changed a little, the beatings and physical humiliation were no longer at their former pitch, but it was still unpleasant. I later learnt that the reason for this fundamental shift in their tactics was the departure of the President and his family on 14 January. The country had entered a new phase. To this day I recall hearing voices like the roaring of a wave. I thought that it must be the buzzing in my ears, but it was the sound of Tunisians chanting, 'Get out! Get out!' outside the Interior Ministry.

It was difficult for me. I was not yet accustomed to my new circumstances: a filthy cell with scratched, blood-smeared walls, a stomach-turning hole in the floor for a lavatory, and dirt everywhere. My only hope of human contact was my two fellow inmates. We spoke to each other very little because we were rarely all together at once: one of us was always being interrogated, sleeping or writhing in pain.

Revolution

I could not believe it when our captors opened the door to take us out, not into the interrogation room this time, but into the breeze of freedom. We were released on 18 January. I was indescribably happy to see my companions again who, despite their injuries, were alive and well. The minutes passed quickly, as in a dream, as they handed us our possessions and our phones and we walked straight from the belly of the Interior Ministry into Avenue Habib Bourguiba. It felt as though we had been squatting in a cave for years before walking out into the light.

Astonished and delighted I called my family and Ezza, and told them that I was free. I heard the cries of joy down the phone and knew that another Tunisia was in the process of being formed. In the heart of the capital, surrounded by my comrades and watched by agents of the Interior Ministry I roared aloud and then, unable to contain myself, burst into tears.

There was a packed reception committee waiting for me in my neighbourhood. I was borne aloft on shoulders and the house heaved with visitors, all of whom wanted to see the young man who had made it out of the ministry's dungeons alive. In my father's eyes I saw joy and pride and this alone was enough to make me glad that my friends and I had played our modest part in the Tunisian people's revolution against their cruel overlords.

At first everyone was on a high: the President's flight abroad, the rapid revolutionary changes imposed by an enthusiastic public, the thundering roar of a people who had risen from beneath the ashes of misery and fear like a phoenix. It was pure romance, and I remember it now with much nostalgia and awe. But then things changed. New balances of power, new circles of influence, new political relationships began to take shape, and it seemed to me, and others like me, that the dictator's departure had not resulted in the departure of dictatorship. Corruption still riddled the body politic and the corrupt themselves, the 'followers of the former regime', still crept through the veins of State agencies, the media and the judiciary.

The fact is that it was almost impossible to take a step back from events in order to evaluate them with the requisite cool-headedness and wisdom. Things were evolving at a lunatic pace, as though history itself were speeding up or condensing. What should rightfully take 20 years to come about was zipping to life in a matter of days. More significantly, everybody was taken by surprise. They were confused.

When I emerged from the cells I found everybody talking about the 'January 14 Revolution' or the 'Jasmine Revolution' or the 'Revolution of the Youth'. I was not keen on reducing the revolutionary process to some event that began on 17 December and ended when the President flew out of the country on 14 January. I was wary of the word 'revolution' itself, not just because true revolution means establishing a new political awareness and creating a break with the past, but also because the most fervent champions of this 'revolution' had been the biggest beneficiaries of Ben Ali's regime. It was as though by riding on the coat-tails of the event and dressing like revolutionaries they were seeking to slow the momentum of the street, sapping its desire to move forward by persuading people that the revolution was over, that their job was done. Yet all the evidence suggested that revolution was a long and tricky road and that this 'process of becoming' must be pushed to its limits, protected at all times and its consciousness firmly implanted in the population.

Tunisians did fight. They embarked upon two epic demonstrations in the Kasbah and engaged in heroic battles on a number of fronts to force the new government to throw out the symbols of the old regime and hold the martyrs' murderers to account. They demanded that a Founding National Council be elected to write a new constitution for the country, a new social and political contract to organize the relationship of society with the State. Thanks to the determination on their part the revolutionary momentum was sustained and their efforts were crowned by the first plural and democratic elections in Tunisia's history.

Prior to this, some close friends of mine founded the New Generation movement, to which end we organized a vast student rally at April 9 college on 28 April 2011, where we released our founding document: 'Who are we, and how do we understand the revolution?' We maintain that the revolutionary process has disoriented traditional thought, which usually nominates other actors to carry out revolutions (such as the working class and its political representatives, the vanguard and the army). It has destroyed the myth of 'Oriental exceptionalism'. We maintain that the revolutionary process is a golden opportunity to renew the social contract and revolutionize its socio-political structures. In its essence it is a formational moment in contemporary political thought, in the current state of international relations and in Arab thought in general.

Through the summer months, against the background of an increasingly complex political and social environment, New Generation pursued its mission within the framework of the Loyal Initiative. The Loyal, or The Youth Movement for Completing the Revolution, is an alliance of various youth movements and independent political actors that seeks to preserve consciousness and awareness in the cities, the neighbourhoods and the young men and women of the revolution. We organized sit-ins and mass protests and spread throughout the country, opening district and municipal branches. Our reputation grew and we developed extensive contacts. We were respected wherever we went.

Today, when I look at the revolution, I note that the youths and district activists who were its original architects are almost entirely absent from public life, when they should be the strongest political force in the land. What made our revolution special is that its leadership remained anonymous, barely visible. But there are many who falsely claim to be leaders. They are only now lifting their heads from the sand where they had been buried like ostriches for the long years of despotism and oppression. From their ivory towers they see fit to give us lectures on patriotism and the struggle. Once firmly in the ranks of the dictatorship they show no shame over their inglorious past but fight like dogs for plum positions, labelling themselves 'experts' or 'analysts'. They work to halt the revolution's progress and divert public opinion towards illusory issues, to make them forget their pain, and numb them with the opiates of eloquence. Which will conquer: the coup or the revolution? The revolutionaries or the opportunists? The 'square' is now the province of political parties and movements with an overwhelmingly sectarian or *identitariste* agenda who promote themselves at the expense of the revolution. The bitter truth is that they have every right to do so. They have reaped what they sowed: how can we begrudge them the chance to stuff their faces and gain some respite from their back-breaking toil in the fields?

Sometimes I feel that all hope is lost. I feel that the wonderful dawn we saw sketched out when the revolution was at its height has gradually faded as events have moved from the street into closed rooms, from public squares ringing with the chants of the angry youth to miked-up podiums and party headquarters, from the barefoot, shirtless crowds confronting their tormentors to well-groomed, scented men in smart suits, smiling for the camera and speaking in the name of an event they were never part of.

The loyal

I am scared, too: scared that a beautiful hope will evaporate away; scared that the dream will not become a reality. I am worried that the political will hijack the debate at the expense of the economic and social. I wonder how will we reconcile the values of political modernism on the one hand and those of our medieval Islamic 'tradition' on the other? How will we solve the tension between issues of cultural specificity and more universal questions? How will we re-enter history after centuries spent on the sidelines? I am worried that we will become confused, or hesitant, or enter into feuds that will distract us from a courageous search for our identity in a diverse and plural world.

I am scared, but it is not the fear of someone who sits on the sofa at home watching the news and reading the papers. It is the fear of the activist; the fear of the young man who never sought to exaggerate the gains made with the blood, sweat and tears of his people. It is the fear that gives me strength, that pushes me to work, forces me to try harder, to give more. It is a positive fear, if that makes sense. I shall not tell you that I am optimistic for the future. I am not. But I believe in the will of the people and remain certain, deep down, that the will of the people will be triumphant. We shall be victorious, quite simply because we have become incapable of losing.

Tunis
November 2011

2

CAIRO, CITY IN WAITING (EGYPT)

By Yasmine El Rashidi

I

If you had asked me that December, just after Christmas, when I would be back, I probably, or most certainly, would have said never. In that month, when the walls seeped cold and the city felt tense from a winter of discomfort, I spent my days filtering through pictures and papers, and odd objects crammed in drawers; fragmented mementos, you could say, that collectively spanned a narrative that was meant to be my life. This was Cairo. My grandmother's house. Some months after my university graduation. Three weeks before my departure. I was leaving Cairo for a fellowship in Washington DC, departing on what I thought was to be my final exit – my first and last goodbye to this city, al-Qahira, *Om al-Dunia.**

I had grown up in this house that my grandmother built along the banks of the River Nile – the same one that my mother and aunts and uncle had grown up in – and in those few days after Christmas and before the New Year, I consumed its every

---

* 'Mother of the World'

corner. I roamed and paced, the bedrooms, the bathrooms, the sitting rooms, the kitchens – all 20-odd rooms, and even the basement. The search, it seemed, was for details – memories, stories, reminders – to store in my mind, somewhere, somehow, just in case, one day, I wanted to remember.

The house at 25a was the only one that still stood on the street, the others had been pulled down over the years and replaced by Soviet-style buildings. From the outside, my grandmother's house, too, was relatively nondescript. Low-lying and linear, it had greyed over the years and been marked by time – scars, where falling trees had clawed as they fell to the ground; veins, of wires that accumulated over the years as technology advanced and new devices were installed; scabs, of dust that had etched itself into walls creating a sepia collage of spheres. There was one particularly large cement-coloured blotch by the bathroom window on the second floor that was visible even from across the street. Guests would sometimes remark on it, asking if there might be a leak.

Many of the rooms of the house were closed by the time I came to depart, shutters down, curtains drawn, furniture covered with sheets and plastic and an additional layer of dust. I opened doors and closed them quickly that winter, entering rooms long abandoned and rushing out, away from the decay, the loss, the sense of the irrevocable. In each of the many closed rooms the musky smell of trapped air left behind from a day long ago intoxicated me, and across the two floors and many rooms, I found myself gravitating to what remained: arrangements of family pictures, and then to the balconies. From the oval kitchen balcony, there was the view of the Chinese embassy and its colony next door; from the main terrace, the front garden; from my mother's bedroom balcony, the neighbouring Russian press, who we were convinced were spies. From my brother's balcony, I looked onto my uncle's house next door; and from my own small bedroom window, the view that I had taken in for 19 consecutive years of my life. It was a view I knew well, and yet, it constantly took me by surprise: where the gentle grass slope once met the Nile, was now a rusty fence, red brick, barbed wire, and a filth-coated government emblem embossed on a steel plaque. Where there had been a mango tree, there were weeds and then white bougainvillea and then pink flowers and then orange ones, and now, just dry soil. Where there had been a lush lawn, many relatives, a menagerie of pets, and a stream of friends running, endlessly, breathlessly, through the day, doing cartwheels, making mud pies, playing games with the dogs, there was now a tired tapestry of woven grass – different shades of green, different shades of gold, different shades of ash. The dogs had gone, and there were seldom any guests. There was also no longer family. Many of them had died. Many more had left. My father even had fled, out of the country and away from the shackles of a system that seemed intent on destruction. I was young when he left, and the details of the story I never fully understood, but I knew, over the years, that they had crushed him. 'He became a broken man,' a relative had said.

This, all of it, what it represented, was the Cairo I was packing from. This was 1997.

* * *

When I first left that Cairo at the turn of the New Year, I packed and dispersed the details of my life with the intent of someone going for good. I had done what I could to make this city work for me, searching in its merciless matrix of nondescript blocks for a space in which I could breathe – a small hole, a crack, a forgotten corner of something to call my own. I wanted a place to belong, and a sense of possibility. Although 19, I was, in my mind, young when I finally gave up. In that abandon of youth, I was distracted by the portrait of America created in my mind's eye and neglected essential details of the Cairo that I would only years later discover were an intrinsic part of who I was. The details of a city that I later came to love as much as loathe. In Washington DC, the first stop of what would become a recurring US sojourn, I survived mere months. Tormented by time zones, I forced myself to stay up in exhausted delirium, through the nights, through the days that became weeks, imagining in detail what was happening, in Cairo, at every hour of every day. What would my mother have been doing then? Where was my brother?

I departed and returned to Cairo many times in the months and years after that. Each time, in the gap between trips, I was reminded that the Cairo I knew, the Cairo I struggled with, the Cairo I tried, repeatedly, to sever myself from, was struggling itself – growing downtrodden and dim.

The signs of decay were everywhere, manifest in the potholed sidewalks and soot-covered buildings. Elaborate stucco adornments were amputated from building facades, once meticulously hand-crafted storefronts of carved wood and hand-painted glass had been replaced with exteriors of raw concrete slabs. Houses had been bulldozed to the ground, monuments were crumbling. Even the Sphinx had lost his nose. Soggy cardboard boxes were thrown outside grocery stores and shops and residential buildings, filled with litter and cigarette stubs and cats, who trawled their way through in the hope of finding something, anything, in this city stricken by despair. Everywhere, it seemed, there were young men, in tight, faux-designer jeans and T-shirts: Levis Straus, Armeni, G&D. They loitered on car hoods smoking cigarettes and watching girls walk by. More and more of those young women, even schoolgirls, were covered by the veil. They too lingered, outside schools, at cafes, on ledges on the banks of the slime-green River Nile. Everywhere, it seemed, there were young people hanging around, milling, smoking cigarettes, smoking water-pipes, staring, somewhere, into oblivion. And there didn't really need to be a sidewalk cafe or a school or a kiosk or sporting club to attract the crowds. Any place where a car could be parked – on the many rows of illegally double- and triple-parked vehicles throughout the city – was an opportunity to loiter, to sit for hours, passing time, until the driver came back, or the heat became too much, or a policeman shouted them away.

Over the years as I travelled back and forth, it seemed as if the population I had known had taken to the streets, out of sheer listlessness; a peaceful expression of 'lack of' – *bidoun*. There was an increasing lack of jobs, of opportunities, of possibilities for a better life. An absence of hope. The government was promising reforms, privatizing, implementing wide-scale programmes intended to boost the economy and improve the quality of life. The indicators suggested that indeed, the future was bright. But the reality, away from the numbers, was abjection; abject poverty, abject despair. Despair so deeply ingested in the psyche of Egyptians it had turned, over the years, into an apathy palpable even in the city's air. In many ways, this was a population inert, sinking deeper and deeper, and I found myself floating, listlessly, restlessly, aimlessly, burdened by my own self, as well as the story of this city. 'It is,' a friend had said once of Cairo, 'like when a person decides to die.'

And yet, even those who decide they are ready to die are sometimes deceived by life itself, and in the story of Cairo, there would be days, sometimes months, when there would suddenly emerge glimmers of some promise of change. The pace would quicken, energy would mount, momentum would build. The odd group of demonstrators demanding economic solutions, or a Palestinian state, or higher wages, would gather in downtown's central Tahrir Square making a ruckus. Sometimes, they would create enough of a disruption to the monotony of daily tedium to attract the media. 'Egypt looks ahead to a portentous year', Mona El-Ghobashy wrote in 2005. 'Egypt's youth have had enough', another newspaper stated that same year. At the peak of those moments – 2005 and 2008 – various groups would unite and protest, somewhat regularly their forceful chants stirring the police to crack down, beat them up and throw them in jail. This was, some said then, the Arab Spring. Yet, away from these protests of a few hundred people (surrounded by twice as many police) that were little more than tiny dots on the map of both Egypt and Cairo, young men, and, increasingly, women, just hung out. Smoking. Skulking. Wading their way through the littered and muddy streets, browsing storefronts that they would never enter, changing ringtones on old Nokia phones, and waiting. Waiting for the evening to unfold into something different, waiting for the possibility of a new life that may present itself in the glimmer of an eye, for the possibility of a romance. But mostly, just waiting – from one day to the next, not for anything in particular except the passing of time. Waiting, in that passing, for something to change.

II

It was in the summer of 2010, that I understood something had in fact shifted. In the people, on the streets, in conversations. It was clear – this was a different Cairo to the one I had left years ago and returned to, for good, in 2008. The year, which started off badly, had turned into a murderous one. It began in the cool breeze of 6 January, when gunmen shot and killed eight Coptic Christians as they were leaving church following Christmas mass. A police report said there was not enough evidence to sentence the three implicated gunmen, and their trial was repeatedly – and over the course of the year – delayed. A few months later, a young man with no history of anything beyond cruising the streets with friends, and the internet for game sites, was picked up by police at an internet cafe on a corner by his house and ferociously beaten to death. Khaled Said was 28. Pictures from the morgue show a disfigured and swollen face: bruised, bloody, with broken teeth. A police report alleges he choked on drugs. It wasn't the first case of its kind, and it wouldn't be the last.

In the meantime, as well as before his death and after it, the country's regime gambled in the currency of lies. Court cases were being overturned, giving leniency to businessmen who had first received death sentences, and corruption cases were swept into government voids, disappearing. Newspaper pages were filling with stories of desperate acts, and by August, with temperatures at all-time highs, inflation soaring, and prices at a peak, it was clear – certainly in the capital Cairo – that we were on the brink of something. The usually jovial Egyptians were angry – bickering and fights punctuated every street corner, taxi drivers were getting out of their cars with increasing regularity, chasing even women, wanting that extra pound. The prime minister, Ahmed Nazif, inflamed the situation by announcing that price control was out of his hands. 'There is nothing I can do,' he announced.

I collected newspaper clippings that summer, dividing them in files. It began inadvertently, perhaps even fortuitously, for when I looked, the thickest of them was an index of crime. A file of 702 clips. It was out of that file that I started to write that summer, in a journal that over time turned into an archive of torture and a record of witnessing a city collapsing:

The man with coloured eyes in apartment number three choked his wife and child and dumped them in a putrid canal on the outskirts of the city. The university graduate jumped in through the window of the seven-bedroom suburban house with three garages and four cars and stabbed a 39-year-old woman, her five-year-old and a Filipino maid, 22 times in total. The father of nine woke up one morning in August eight weeks ago, left home for his job frying food at a local kiosk, and has not been seen since.

The Egyptian pound plummeted against the dollar and prices went up. The summer was the hottest the city had witnessed in 50 years. Air-conditioners dripped water onto sidewalks and chugged until they choked and broke down. Temperatures soared and humidity settled in the narrow alleys and over the urban skyline, turning the dusty air into a murky veil. By mid-summer, power outages consistently gripped the city, and labourers marched onto the highways on urban fringes, irate. For the first time in decades, the Holy month of Ramadan fell during August. Officials were in a quandary. With sunset at past 7 p.m., they fretted about what people may do without food or water in this ominous heat. Behind closed doors and in consultation with Islamic scholars, it was decided that for one month the clocks would change. The fast would be broken one hour earlier. For a single month in August, the government would manipulate time, lessening the wait.

But even GMT+4 did little to help. When the power short-circuited and fridges and fans broke down, the usual cacophony of people and cars pouring through the city's already-clogged arteries intensified and turned frenetic. Workers staged strikes. University students staged sit-ins. Taxi drivers belched profanities. Islamic scholars sermonized about composure, offering lessons on how the suffering of this summer would be rewarded in the after-life. Mosque speakers were amplified and preachers shrieked into the skies at all hours of the day and night. Paradise awaits, they called.

State-owned media reported temperatures to be between 39 and 41 degrees centigrade, but on every sidewalk people muttered it was 50 degrees today. It could well have been if one measured temperature by the count of sweat beads dripping from the forehead of the bearded taxi driver in a pale blue shirt now patch-worked with sweat. He pressed down on his horn for a continuous beep from the beginning of the tree-lined street along the Nile, until its end, two kilometres later. Qur'anic verses blasted from his cassette player and he mumbled to himself, shaking his hand jarringly at the female driver swerving between lanes. *'Allah yikhrib beitik,'* he swore. *'Allah yikhrib beit al-hukuma wil-harr.'* The heat. The government and the heat, he cursed.

On a speech-writing assignment for Egypt's First Lady in the weeks preceding that summer, I had been asked to redraft my copy to include mention of 'climate change', notably, the ruling family's effort and continued commitment to combat global warming. 'Mention it at least a few times,' they said. 'And stress our work on poverty alleviation.' In that same week, my mother's cook, a wiry woman with greying hair, calloused hands and a face not dissimilar to a Persian cat, threatened to take the President and his wife and the Prime Minister and slice them thinly with a butcher's knife, like the roast being cut for dinner. My mother called me, worried. 'The government is driving people to the edge,' she said, '*Rabina yustor*.' ('God be Merciful.')

People wished August away with fervor. By day eight of the 31 days of the Holy month of Ramadan, even the most devout of the pious Muslims I knew were wishing it to end. Moods were low. Food prices had risen since the start of the summer, and a general sense of frustration overshadowed the usual social festivities of this month. At dinner tables people mostly grumbled about the heat. Then wondered aloud about the President. If he was really still alive, if he would ever yield. What would happen next.

We all waited. We waited for something to change.

* * *

Soon after that summer, ahead of the parliamentary elections in November, the crackdowns began: press freedoms were curbed, campaigning techniques stifled and outlawed, and scores of opposition members were rounded up and thrust in jail. The elections themselves, when they happened, were ruthless – witness to a regime's security apparatus run amok. The result, aside from injuries and deaths and kidnappings at the hands of State security agents and thugs, was a sweeping win by Mubarak's ruling National Democratic Party (NDP). I wrote a story for a local paper at the time about *Thugs for Hire*. Many of those I interviewed pointed the finger at NDP men, whose campaign expenditures were on average 1,000 times higher than the LE100,000 ceiling legally stipulated. We all understood that the stakes in these elections were higher than ever before: in the coming year was a presidential election, and the NDP would be doing all it could to manoeuvre Gamal Mubarak into a position where he could swiftly rise to power as leader of the State, taking over from his father's 30 year rule. Although there was talk that the military were against him, and we all deduced and theorized that they may stage a coup, 'Jimmy's' only chance at the presidential throne was in his father's lifetime – the parliamentary elections were the necessary juncture: only a sweeping NDP win could secure his plans. The opposition was pulverized by the NDP and the public voice obliterated. Minority groups cried foul, saying they had been all but annihilated, and once somewhat pacified liberal politicians and parties were outraged. The government had created perhaps its greatest ever cohort of aggrieved politicians, and they swiftly called the elections a sham, swearing they would not let the NDP or the octogenarian Mubarak get away with this political fiction.

Tension was mounting. In an article the week of the election results, I wrote:

The opposition have stepped up to denounce the current political predicament, saying that the violence that marred this year's elections could well continue – this time from a nation outraged at an establishment they view as tyrannical. Activists and human rights groups have said the regime is pushing a people to their limits, echoing suggestions of impending unrest.

Several months later, when a suicide bomber struck a church in Alexandria on New Year's Eve – killing 23 and injuring over 80 – it was one of the final few straws for a population with many gripes against a government meant to serve and protect them. The State-owned newspapers ran contradictory stories each day about the suicide bomber and the details of the story (it was a car bomb, no it was a suicide bomber, no he was a 30-something-year-old Afghan fighter en route from Iraq to the Maghreb, no he was an Egyptian youth from the Nile Delta) raising ire in the public sphere. Muslims and Copts alike pointed the accusatory finger at the regime, implicating it in both this and other recent incidents of sectarian strife. Spontaneously, Muslims and Christians united, and on the eve of Coptic Christmas on 6 January, Muslims – myself included – turned up in droves, offering their bodies, and lives, to the embattled minority community. We attended church services, surrounded churches as symbolic 'human shields' and raised the symbol of an Egypt for All: the cross within the crescent.

People were coming together. Change was in the air. Just days later, in January, at protests in solidarity with insurrection-afflicted Tunisia, once disparate groups united in amplified protest, their grievances – once separate – were in many ways now just one: against a regime. I spent days and evenings on the streets, demonstrating, lingering, speaking to people about their problems and stories and struggles. Conversations were charged. On 11 January, for the local web-based English language daily paper, *AhramOnline*, I wrote:

Egypt's youth activist population are itching to revolt [...] In an ominous turn, Egyptian activists have declared solidarity with Tunisian rioters [...] The cumulative discontent of the elections, the religious persecution, and the long-standing economic troubles that plague the majority of the nation's 80 million population, may very well unite disparate groups, bringing them together in a larger, more forceful movement for change.

III

Some say it began three years ago, and others, that the revolution has been in the making for ten. As narrated by the media and analysts, the story of the new Egypt – and the people of Egypt who revolted – might have begun 30 years ago, when Hosni Mubarak came to power. For a few, the story began just seven years ago, when a movement for change, Kefaya, was formed; or maybe one day in 2011 when a Google executive created a Facebook page called We are All Khaled Said. For others, the story began on 6 April 2008 when Esraa Abdel Fattah, a 27-year-old moonlighting as an activist, mobilized 30,000 Egyptians into the streets in a protest in solidarity with striking textile workers in the industrial city of Mahalla. Esraa, who had received an SMS some two weeks before from a worker who intended to strike, had been lying in bed one day in late March with a blinding headache. 'I knew I wanted to help, I knew the conditions of these workers were bad. I knew it was up to people like me, like us, to do something. I just didn't know how. It was making me sick,' she told me.

Esraa paced that day. She paced for hours, getting into bed occasionally and putting her hand on her forehead as she closed her eyes to try to ease the pain. Her own version of the story has varied slightly, but at approximately 4 p.m., she got up for a coffee and what would be her single meal that day: a sandwich of white cheese and butter in a palm-sized loaf of white Egyptian bread. And then at 5.30 p.m., it happened. As she sat down to her computer and logged into her several-months-old Facebook account, the idea clicked. 'I would create a Facebook page,' she said. 'It came to me in a flash. I would call on Egyptians to strike on 6 April 2008, in solidarity with underpaid labourers.' (6 April 1930 was the day Gandhi, after walking for 241 miles on foot from his village to the sea, raised a lump of salty mud and declared, 'With this, I am shaking the foundations of the British Empire.')

What happened in the days following has been widely documented by the media – the April 6 Facebook page amassed 70,000 supporters in the space of a week, the ensuing protests were the largest the country had seen, and Esraa was detained and jailed for 18 days on charges of threatening the security of the State and inciting violence and anarchy. In her honour and as a statement of solidarity, a group of her friends formed the 'April 6 group' to lobby for her release. In many ways, that moment – her epiphany, the creation of the Facebook page, the conception of the April 6 Movement – was indeed the start of the revolution. But so is the date of the appointment of Mubarak, and so was the formation of the first movement for change, Kefaya, and so are the protests that escalated in 2005, and the fraudulent parliamentary elections of 2010, and the church bombing of the following month. And so was, too, the rise of Gamal Abdel Nasser some five decades earlier. There is, in the end, no single moment, no single event, no single person. There are both events and predicaments – a cultural and social fabric, an economic reality, an urban landscape – that all came together in the making of the Egypt that has weighed down on many of us for years.

* * *

The new force of that movement for change became evident on Friday, 28 January 2011, just after midday prayer. It continues as I write this now – 2 May 2011 – and as I do, my one thought, the most significant factor amidst it all, is that my relationship with this city, with a culture, with my home, has forever been changed, and that my memories of the 18 days, the revolution, are mere fragments of a larger journey and search that I now wait to complete.

Those fragments – the memories of a revolution – are many.

There were the riot police, who pulled down their face masks and moved forward. Their batons were raised high, their shields above their chests. They charged, hundreds of them, grabbing people by the scruff of their necks, kicking them, beating them down hard. Many were dragged away, into narrow side-streets, disappearing. My friend Mohamed vanished, to resurface many days later.

There was the metal canister, which rocketed up into the air, exploding into volcanic fumes. It spiralled down, leaving a helix of trailing smoke that settled, eventually, over the square. It was followed by another, and another, and another. Someone said they fired 50 in a row. Many people fell to the ground, choking. My own eyes were filled with tears that felt like blood. I wondered if I would be able to see again. If I would survive.

There was the young woman, whose body was limp. They carried her out, her blood on their hands, screaming for help. 'Anyone, please, an ambulance, an ambulance.' There were none, and a young man dropped to his knees by her side, sobbing. She was his sister. She had begged to go out that day, and he had promised his parents she would come to no harm.

There were the sounds of bullets assaulting the chants of the crowds. Two men came sprinting from around the corner, their faces gripped with terror. 'It's real, it's real. Live ammunition, they're using live ammunition.' No one knew if it was true – we had heard this before. Minutes later, a procession with three bodies was carried into the square. One, of a young child. Thousands kneeled down in prayer.

There was the girl with braided pigtails and a pink dress who carried a flag twice her size. She must have been seven, and was happy that school had been closed. She begged her father for more popcorn, but before he had a chance to answer, she had already lost herself in animated chants. '*Howa yimshi, mish hanimshi!*' ('He should leave, we're not leaving!')

There was a boy in a mustard-yellow Adidas hoodie who wore a circus-clown wig – red, white and black, the colours of the Egyptian flag. He also carried a sign telling Mubarak to 'Get lost – we deserve change.' He was 18, and said he cared nothing about politics, or his country, until then. Before this, he told me, his life was about studying and 'getting the hell out'.

There was the moment when opposition party member Mounir Fakhri Abdel Nour navigated his way through the protesters surrounded by bodyguards. He wore a pale blue shirt and a tweed blazer. People wanted to shake his hand, to take his picture, to share with him ideas. 'This is just the beginning,' he told a woman in her seventies. 'Everyone will have a chance to speak. All voices will be heard. I assure you of that.' The woman's eyes glistened with tears.

There was the man with missing teeth who sat on a sidewalk, writing. Page after sketchbook page of Arabic script. His slogans and poems and essays told tales of corruption and vice. He had been in that same spot for two weeks and said he would stay until the day he died. 'I carry the emotion of a nation, not only my own.'

There was the novelist Ahdaf Soueif, who carried three bulging nylon bags, hanging on her arm. Cookies and small savoury pastries. 'I come every day,' she said, dipping into one bag. She wore dark sunglasses, but they did little to conceal who she was. Crowds gathered around her, all with stories of struggle. They asked her to give them voice. She listened, for hours, and promised to help.

There was always the mother of Khaled Said, who one day walked onto 'Liberation' stage in Tahrir Square. She held a picture of her son. 'My son's blood, and that of the martyrs of this square, will not be lost in vain. We will not give up. We will not give up. We will not give up.' The crowd erupted into roars of applause, echoing her words.

And then there were the friends.

A friend, long housebound, ridden with depression, said he felt reborn. I saw him every day in the square, marching, chanting, and when it was over, dancing in the streets, holding his head up high.

A dancer friend cancelled a performance in Europe to remain in Egypt and take part in the protests.

An artist friend cancelled a lecture series in New York.

A writer friend flew back from Los Angeles, and a filmmaker friend from DC.

A friend who fled Egypt 22 years ago vowing never to return, came back, on day eight. She decided it was time.

And there was my mother, a fragile woman who is uncomfortable in crowds and had watched the protests unfold with fear on TV, who told me one day that she wanted to come out and march as well. She had been moved to tears by the story of Google executive Wael Ghonim, and by the stories of those killed.

My father and I spoke at least three times a day in those days of the revolution. Ours had been a decade of strained contact. We reconciled, and then bonded, over a city – ours.

***

To look back on those days – to remember – is to reflect on 18 days that I sense we may live in the shadow of for years to come. I watched people fall to the ground, gasping their last breaths. I fell to the ground myself, choking on tear gas. We dodged bullets and ran from armed men. We taped our windows with newspapers and formed barricades around our homes. My mother's porter attached a kitchen knife to a broomstick and took to the streets. He said he would die protecting her, with his spear. Many of us helped wipe the blood pouring from young men's heads. For the first time in our lives, some of us saw dead bodies lying on the streets. I tried to pry out a bullet from beneath a friend's skin. We ran for cover, from rocks, from Molotov cocktails, from thugs. We became paranoid. We no longer knew whose side a stranger was on. And might he be armed? I had seen many knives stuck in many belts and trouser pockets. I had seen many guns, too. It took us a while to get used to the sight of the army and men with weapons on our streets. For days, we didn't know if they would shoot.

We waited, each day, for something to happen, for something to change. We waited, for hours, as well, for the President to speak.

To look back on those days, is also to look into a new archive of images and a reservoir of emotions that I never thought – until January 2011 – I would ever bear witness to. Cairo, to me, was a city overwhelmed, a city so mammoth in its proportions. Into its sepia-toned landscape, its 20 million people would slip, through dark alleyways, to be forgotten by a world around them that seemed stark of possibilities. This Cairo that I lived in spared no one, and everywhere I turned, every corner of every street I knew, there were intimations of struggle. Even my house seemed to have grown weary, as burdened and sad and oppressed as a greying building can be.

In those 18 days that have come to be known as the 'Egyptian revolution', as I navigated my way between my grandmother's house – which had become home again some four years before – and Tahrir Square, I watched something, very slowly, transform. The street-side vendor suddenly had an Egyptian flag; the taxi driver had an opinion; the young man on the street was no longer scared to say that there was something he didn't like; the tree trunks were painted red, white and black; the youth, once skulking, were now handing out flyers, forming political parties and collectives, chanting, discussing, planning, hoping, for those better lives. For every emotion, every thought, every idea, now, there was an audience, and on the same street corners that were once host to dejection, possibility was being born. I watched, in the days of the Egyptian uprising and the months that followed, human emotion finding an outlet, and in tandem discovering its source. I witnessed, in the waiting time of those days until 5.56 p.m. on 11 February, dignity restored. In myself, too.

IV

I bumped into my neighbour at the supermarket the other day. A retired Gulf Air executive, he had been active on Facebook during the uprising when protesters occupied Tahrir Square. I hadn't seen or spoken to him since, and his warnings, posted on my Facebook wall, were always left unanswered.

'Yas,' he said, taking my hand, shaking it.

'You know,' he said, half smiling, half serious, his face pale, 'it was very risky what you did, by the way.'

I must have looked puzzled.

'This business of going down to Tahrir,' he offered. 'Very high risk.'

I laughed.

'You could have been killed. Your poor Mom. What were you thinking?'

'Well, we got rid of the President!' I retorted.

'Well,' he said, 'let's see if things improve. You know, the economy has taken a big blow, Yasmine. People need jobs. Life is hard.'

'And I just hope you guys are going to take care of these Salafists and Islamists now,' he continued, slowing down, taking in my own slight nod of acknowledgement.

'You know, we're all waiting to see,' he said, closing the conversation and walking away.

Cairo
May 2011

3

BAYOU AND LAILA (LIBYA)

By Mohamed Mesrati
Translated from the Arabic by Robin Moger

I

Twenty years ago in Tripoli I was born into history. The country was suffering under merciless international sanctions imposed in the wake of the Lockerbie bombing and the weather was sweltering. I spent my early years learning to dance to cartoon soundtracks and then I went to school.

On my first day my teacher slapped me because I couldn't memorize a small verse of the Qur'an. I remember her telling me, 'You're a donkey!' and to this day, whenever anyone uses that word I am reminded of my introduction to the world of learning.

From that day forward I would either fail or be sent home with 'borderline' marks, ready and prepared for my father's explosion of rage, my mother's slaps and the disapproving murmurs of uncles and aunts whose children excelled, through bribery. I once asked my father why he didn't give my maths teacher some money so I could pass and he whacked me.

From this brief summary you can see that my early life was mainly comprised of verbal abuse, smacks and parental tantrums. In other words, it was a pretty normal childhood.

A friend in London, where I ended up in 2009, once told me, 'If your grades at university are as good as they say you must have been one of the top students back home in Libya.'

What he didn't understand is that I could never do well in Libya: I was unable to memorize the Qur'an, I couldn't afford a bribe and I feared the teacher's cane.

As the exams approached, while other students sat up all night studying, wobbly and nauseous with exhaustion, I would be lost in daydreams. One day I was going to leave Tripoli and travel from Libya to London, where I would take a London girl as my lover to keep me warm.

That's right. That was my very first dream, and it came true. And so will all the others – all my wishes, desires, dreams and ambitions: they will all come true.

Libya was never a homeland to me, just a country where I was born and where I lost my innocence. In England I breathed freedom. In London I found myself in the arms of a woman I loved, but who did not return my affection.

***

I'm no artist, but here's a funny story about something that happened to me once.

Art was a second tier subject at school: just a sketchbook in which we illustrated tragic and deeply dull themes like 'Spring', 'The Joy of the Libyan People at the Revolution' or 'Cleansing the British Camps from the Homeland's Soil'. Not once were we asked to draw a loved one's face or our parents. My friends and I, however, were highly skilled at drawing penises on the schoolmistress's chair and deep was my satisfaction whenever she sat down. I was, furthermore, commander of the squad that painted the giant green cock penetrating a vagina on the blackboard, because of which the entire class was punished.

Khairi, Altakali, Baaisho, Faris and I grew up together. Drawing the penis and vagina on the board was Khairi's idea.

Our plan was that the lesson after break would be taken up with interrogating pupils instead of teaching them maths.

At break time we stole green paint from the building adjoining the school's playground and crept into the classroom. Faris and Khairi stood outside pretending to hold a conversation while keeping an eye on people walking by. The rest of us got to work inside. Altakali held the stepladder and Baaisho and I climbed up to paint the penis and vagina and when we had finished we jumped down and called out to the guards outside. Sidling out we carried our equipment to the bathroom and – taking care not to get any on ourselves – we poured paint all over the floor and walls. Then we laughed, slapped hands and went out to play.

***

I was never one for marches. We were a generation born from our fathers' defeats, a generation that first opened its eyes on a society that spoke in the language of oppression, where fear was an unalterable and undeniable destiny. It was a society that for decades had only ever been addressed through blood and death, through the murderous purges of all those who found themselves on the traitors' list. Marches meant nothing to us. We marched at every new flare-up in Gaza and we marched whenever the Brother Leader addressed us on the subjects of imperialism and Zionism, every speech filled with the selfsame words and phrases: enemy, reactionary beliefs, rats, the Green March, the flight to the south, revolution, revolutionary courts, a time to work and a time to march.

Unfortunately, the receiver in our television, and all its channels, were controlled by Gaddafi and his government. Whenever the Brother Leader, or as I call him, Big Brother, came out to address his people the 20 channels became one, dedicated to the pronouncements of the Jamahiriyan Confucius. We would listen to every last word of the historic speech then go back to mindless entertainment.

One spring day in 2003 Tripoli's secondary school students were sent out on a march to Martyrs' Square. We were delighted, because we would be spared the maths teacher punishing us for our inability to solve basic quadratic equations, and we were alert for the slightest opportunity to escape the watchful eyes of the soldiers who surrounded us, ready to slip down the nearest alley and go to the sea to swim.

On the day of a march we would usually gather in the playground for the headmaster to give a little speech about whatever it was, then set off chanting in praise of Gaddafi's revolution (his coup, that is), portraits of Big Brother and banners daubed with his sayings held aloft. 'Stand firm, stand firm, lone falcon!' we would scream: 'Teach us, O leader, teach us how to attain our destiny!' We'd go wild, kicking each other and jumping around. At Martyrs' Square, where the pupils of all the city's schools were packed together as tight as nuts in chocolate, we would rush to claim a place next to the girls from Jamila College, elegant and beautiful with their alluring smiles. We pressed up next to them chanting loudly to show that next to our patriotic duty they were less than nothing. Luckily I was skinny and always managed to slip through the crowd until I got in amongst the girls, where, like everyone else, my questing fingers poked and prodded in every direction.

That day in 2003 was boiling. As I sit here writing I can still feel the April heat of that city, set between the chill of the ocean and the desert's dust. I was with those four dearest friends – Baaisho, Khairi, Munir and Altakali – and we were shouting out words and slogans that meant nothing to us, abusing the Americans, the British, and imperialism and praising Big Brother whose portraits we could see on the skyscrapers and bank buildings around us. The chanting didn't interest us half as much as the prospect of escaping this slow advance on Martyrs' Square and ducking down a narrow passageway that would lead us to Mizran Street. Turning to Baaisho I whispered: 'What do you say we wait until al-Wahshi Alley. It'll take us to Belkhair Square.'

As we entered the alley we heard someone shout, 'Hey, you animals! Where do you think you're going? Come here.' We walked faster. When footsteps began to follow us I clutched at my heart and surged forward shouting, '*Ouuuma!*' a Tripolitan street cry derived from Italian, used to warn of impending danger, and as they raced along behind me, my friends called with me.

By the Ben Naji Mosque, Khairi said we should split up and meet later at Cafe Sinbad. I went down a small alley next to the mosque that brought me to the car park where the African car washers work. From time to time I turned around, worried about the soldier who'd been chasing us and, reaching the Haiti Street crossroad, I caught my breath and set out at a walking pace for the Karshoud Mosque and the internet cafe called Sinbad that stood nearby. When I got there I took a computer and sat down to browse porn sites until my friends arrived.

**

I used to feel like a hero – but not for escaping one of Gaddafi's marches. The moment I left Libya for England in mid-2005 with my siblings and parents I tasted freedom and for me it was a gift not to be wasted. Every day, morning or afternoon, I sat at my laptop typing out letters by the hundred, words by the dozen, pouring scorn on the regime and recounting the tale of its blood-spattered past. I grew up in a family that was open-minded and believed in freedom, and this is what enabled me to write, to criticize the Libyan regime, to curse and abuse it as I saw fit. In the evening I would go to the pub with my new friends. We drank glass after glass and talked of political systems and dictatorships, and I would tell them about my experiences as a Libyan from a family that suffered from Gaddafi's injustice. Then we would part ways, tumbling from the bar delighted with our conversation and promising to meet again.

The day I left Libya was no normal day. It was strange; I wasn't ready for it. I had heard my father say that we were to leave Libya, but I didn't know why. I longed to see England, but the trip came as a surprise.

Once abroad I made no great effort to call my friends and relatives. You could call it selfishness. I set the past aside; I resolved to change myself. The past was an irritation: poverty; the injustices of the classroom; my father's absence from home; relatives who had all the money they needed, who could walk into any restaurant or club they chose in order to eat and drink to their hearts' content and smoke the most expensive brands of cigarette and finest *narghile* tobacco.

In the UK I felt like a human being. My father didn't have to be some influential government official or businessman. I could go to a police station and lodge a complaint against anybody who had violated my rights, no matter how powerful. I could read any book I wanted without fear of prying eyes. In short: I could have the freedom my parents and I had always dreamt of. Or so I thought.

Naturally, for any new arrival from distant shores such self-respect and dignity will be hard won. First, we had to put up with the employees of the UK Border Agency. The first time I went to the Border Agency's offices in Liverpool I felt I was in the grip of a terrible sickness. I didn't see a single smile all day and no one seemed to understand or appreciate the persecution we had been subjected to in Libya. The official who talked to my family was cold and unresponsive, apparently regarding us as a rabble of refugees who wanted to colonize his country. And of course, having trekked to the Border Agency's offices and spent a whole day filling in forms, scurrying back and forth between officials' desks and being interviewed, our request for political asylum was turned down. My father brought a court case against them, the original decision was upheld and we appealed. It took us three years to receive political asylum.

The times I baulked at studying or refused to leave the house my father would tell me, 'This is your chance. If I'd come to this country at your age I wouldn't be in the state I am now. This place will help you to write and create. Don't let the opportunity slip between your fingers. Make something of yourself and grab it.'

II

Bayou and Laila

The Elephant, O Ruler of Time! was my favourite story when I was a child. On Eid nights my father would tell of the king who owned a huge elephant that he let loose on his kingdom to frolic and play, razing the houses, destroying the markets and killing the people. The inhabitants of the kingdom agreed amongst themselves to go to the king and complain about the elephant's reckless behaviour, then settled down to rehearse their complaint.

One of their number, a man called Zakariya, was to say: 'The elephant, O ruler of time ...' and the throng behind him would passionately cry, '... has brought down our houses.'

'The elephant, O ruler of time ...' Zakariya would say again, and the people would angrily declare, '... has laid waste our fields and spoiled our crops.'

'The elephant, O ruler of time ...' Zakariya would say a third time and the people would exclaim in disgust, '... has wrecked our streets and ruined our children.'

The kingdom's inhabitants rehearsed this complaint for many moons, growing ever more enthusiastic and excited with every day that passed. They cried out their lines, filled with anguish at the injustice they suffered, in a state of constant anticipation of the moment they would go to meet the king and present their case.

Then, one day, they set out.

When they reached the palace the people filed into the king's presence, with Zakariya leading the way.

'The elephant, O ruler of time!' he cried.

The king asked them why they had come.

The people looked at one another then turned their eyes to Zakariya, who swallowed in trepidation and said in a defeated voice, 'The elephant, O ruler of time …'

From the people came nothing but an awful silence and palpable fear.

'The elephant, O ruler of time …' said Zakariya, his legs trembling.

The crowd remained silent, looking at each other and waiting for someone to state their case to the king.

Zakariya turned to the people, saw the fear in their eyes and hissed at them, 'The elephant, O ruler of time …'

Tired of waiting, the king bellowed at Zakariya and the mob to explain what they wanted with the elephant and why they kept repeating his name. Turning to face the king, Zakariya bowed his head and in a broken voice, declared, 'The elephant, O ruler of time, is lonely. We have come to ask you to find him a mate to enrich his life and bear him children.'

The king gave a loud laugh and said to the assembled people, 'It is for this that you have come to me? Very well, as you wish. Bring the elephant a mate of middle age that they may live together.'

And so it came to pass. The she-elephant bore her companion a multitude of little elephants that quickly grew, while the people went on with their rehearsals, crying, 'The elephant, O ruler of time!'

With his rich radio voice and his theatrical gestures, my father, Bayou Mesrati, would tell us the tale of the elephant and when he was finished I would laugh, though something inside me told me that this was a tale to inspire sadness, not laughter. At the time, I was yet to hear of black comedy, but the melancholy behind my father's smile was plain to see. I remember him covering me with the blanket and leaving me to sleep.

In those early years I'd grow dreamy and distracted whenever the story came to mind. It was a constant source of fascination, a perplexing riddle my mind was unable to grasp: a king, an elephant and fearful subjects. My father wasn't around much for me to question him about it; he was always out in the oilfields. For three weeks he would be working in Brega and the oilfields, then after returning home to spend a week with the family he would leave us once again.

In those days my father had given up on culture and the theatre, his sole concern the work that put food on the table for his wife and three children. He was a Libyan, after all: a Libyan whose stage productions had earned him a record of opposition activism. His monthly income was meagre compared to the poorly qualified workers who came from East Asia, Europe and America. Though my father had graduated from university with honours and had an MA to his name with a diploma from a minor petroleum engineering institute he earned less than a British or Japanese labourer and he was frequently driven to take acting jobs on the radio or in short films shown on TV. This work, especially the shows broadcast during Ramadan, enabled him to give his children a joyful Eid and exercise the theatrical talents he had let wither after Gaddafi and his dictatorial regime deprived him of the freedom to nurture a creative, progressive spirit in Libyan theatre.

My father would often praise God for his petroleum qualification. If it weren't for that qualification, he would assert, he would have been forced to spend a lifetime in theatre under a dictatorship that shaped the artist into a mouthpiece of the regime. This is what he left the theatre to avoid, leaving the stage to stay out of the limelight.

***

In 1976 my father put on his first production at the university theatre. Though not yet a student himself he had moved in student theatre circles from the age of 16 as he was friends with an older group that included the founders of the theatre. This was at the University of Tripoli, known under Gaddafi as al-Fatih University, al-Fatih meaning The Liberator in honour of his coup of September 1969. Each and every performance was subject to severe censorship by military appointees without the slightest interest in culture, art or drama. The drama students, my father among them, were delighted with the script they were going to perform. The text itself was an adaptation of some foreign play whose name my father can no longer remember and after long, hard weeks of preparation, rewriting and rearrangement the group were satisfied with what they had. A few weeks before the play was due to go on the university's administration asked them to submit the script to the censor and obtain official approval for the show to go ahead. The play was in five acts and about 100 pages long; the fruit of many hours' rehearsal. They handed it in to the censor's office and after waiting about a month it came back reduced to a single act play of 15 pages.

My father was forever telling me about the socially conscious theatre he believed in, about social criticism and the deconstruction of power; about Syrian playwright Saadallah Wannous, iconic political figure and critic of authority and dictatorship, whose works filled his library; and about many other plays and novels, both Arab and international. When he decided to relocate his book collection from his parent's house into our cramped family home I looked through his old volumes. The margins of most were filled with notes written in pen. When jotting down his thoughts or scribbling notes in books, my father always used a pen. I once asked him why he had written all over his books and he told me that he had been preparing some plays based on the novels and scripts in his collection. I asked him if he had ever put any of them on and he waved his hand dismissively. One or two; the rest were just plans, dreams.

On 7 April* 1976 Abdessalam Jalloud, Gaddafi's right-hand man and the most bestially cruel of the Free Officers, entered the university campus, his gun in his belt and a few guards and henchmen following at his heels. In the main hall he delivered his famous line:

> We shall not be celebrating the 7th of April with fireworks, festivals and parties, but with blood and by purifying the country of agents and traitors.

As he spoke gallows were being erected in the university squares and opponents of the regime, convicted of high treason for nothing more than holding beliefs inconsistent with those of the Brother Leader, were led out to be executed.

This day, and the killings, hangings and purges that preceded it, transformed my parents' and grandparents' generations into a lumpen mass saturated with a fear of death and indiscriminate murder, a paralysed people in a land ruled by a bunch of militias and gangs, a land that knew no law: neither civil courts, nor political parties, nor difference or diversity of opinion. After Colonel Gaddafi and his cronies came to power all symbols of national identity vanished and Libya became a country friendless and fettered.

On the very same date in 1982 my father and a group of drama students were getting ready to perform *Dracula* at the university theatre. They had arranged to meet early for one last rehearsal before the first show, which was scheduled for that afternoon, and they spent the morning cloistered in the small room they used for rehearsals. That afternoon, just before they went on stage, the students received a letter ordering them to cancel the performance for reasons of security. Vehicles arrived bearing timber and rope. Students from the revolutionary committees raided the classrooms and

---

* 7 April was a public holiday created by Gaddafi to celebrate and police the eradication of colonialism and imperialism.

lecture halls and bundled Leftists out to the scaffolds set up in the university's squares. My father witnessed these executions and decided to flee with his friends before it occurred to the killers to claim them too.

But as my father got ready to go to bed that night, revolutionary committee members burst into the house and took him and some other students to a security facility where they were interrogated about the play they were to have performed that day. My father told me that he almost died of fright. He knew that somewhere there was a rope waiting for him. They tried explaining the play to the officer, telling him that it was based on an internationally renowned work, that there was no hidden message being conveyed, that it was no different to when they had put on *Hamlet* and *Macbeth* or any of the other masterpieces of world literature. The story had appealed to them and they simply wanted to entertain people with it, not to make a point. After several days in prison my father was released. He kept himself to himself for a while then re-emerged to join the Free Theatre, a group of Libyan actors and dramatists who had decided to abjure all foreign plays in favour of writing populist theatre that directly engaged with society.

In the ideology of the Brother Leader, foreign meant imperialist, and thus constituted a betrayal of the revolution.

On that day, 7 April 1982, as my father stood gazing at the bodies hanging from the scaffold, my mother, Laila al-Houni, was standing on the other side of the square with her school friends. She was 14.

She and her friends had been told that a circus was visiting the university in celebration of 7 April. Arriving at the university they saw pupils from schools all over the capital city. They all sat on the ground and waited for the show to begin. When the trucks began to arrive carrying the poles for the scaffold they were told it was circus equipment. Soldiers and revolutionary committee members fanned out and the schoolchildren tried escaping over the walls. The men from the revolutionary committees began grabbing anyone they suspected of being politically affiliated to a group opposed to the ideas of Gaddafi. It was easy to spot the soldiers and committee members back then: they styled their hair in an afro to resemble Gaddafi, and made sure to wear clothes that looked like military fatigues – a green linen shirt, black boots that reached to the knee.

My father said there had been rumours that a conflict would break out between the students and the revolutionary committees like the one in 1976, which had left an entire generation of student intellectuals behind bars alongside writers, poets and artists. Fear was everywhere in the square. Most students were trying to sneak past the soldiers and make it over the walls.

My father and his friends started ripping up the books they kept in their small rehearsal room and burned a few. When the opposition activists and students were brought out and pushed onto the scaffold the revolutionaries began hurling abuse at them, shouting Gaddafi's name and his slogans as though they were appointed guardians of some god and his religion.

Of what happened next my mother remembers only a hurricane of hangings, abuse and sobbing, girls fainting and dropping to the ground, women from the revolutionary committees yanking down on the legs of the executed men to make sure they were dead.

***

For my father it was Libya that George Orwell described in *1984*.

It was in Ramadan of that very year that the tyrant perpetrated one of his most horrific crimes, executing opponents in the public squares and plazas and broadcasting their deaths on television to a nation sitting down to break the fast.

Orwell's book was visible on my father's shelves. I can still recall its plain cover and yellowed pages, its solemn black typeface and its stacked lines of close-packed words. My father once advised me to read it. This was back in 2003, when I was 13, and it had never occurred to me to touch a book so old and battered. I often hesitated over it, but it was only in the summer of 2009 that I read it for the first time, urged by my friend, the Libyan author Ghazi Gheblawi, who described it as a perfect analysis of the Libyan condition. I bought it and sat reading for two whole days: Orwell had painted a picture of Libya under Gaddafi. Naturally, I understood that wasn't his intention; he was aiming at every totalitarian regime that overthrows a legitimate government beneath the banner of 'revolution' and commits its crimes and perpetrates terrorism under cover of 'revolutionary law'.

If I had read it back when I was 13 would I have understood why my father wanted me to read it, or would I have raced through it, blissfully unaware, as though reading any other novel or play?

The same thing happened with *The Elephant, O Ruler of Time!* Though it sometimes made me weep when I was young I considered it no more than an entertaining story. Then one day in the winter of 2006 as I sat watching the news with my father, something in our conversation reminded us of the story and the play adapted from it by Saadallah Wannous.

My father explained his understanding of the play and why he had told me the story. The king, he always imagined to be Muammar Gaddafi himself and the elephant, the revolutionary committees, the militias run by the Colonel and his regime, which murdered and pillaged and abducted in the name of 'revolutionary law'. They were the instrument with which Gaddafi ruled the land.

After leaving the theatre my father appeared in a few television dramas but by the early 1990s he had given that up as well. He loathed the recording studios festooned with portraits of Gaddafi; it made his skin crawl to linger in a television building that resembled nothing so much as a secret police headquarters; above all, he hated filming late in the evening. At 10 o'clock, he told me, as they were recording their scenes a gaggle of directors and cameramen would burst in and without asking permission start gathering up cameras and lighting equipment to carry them off to the news studio, all the while shouting, 'The news! The Brother Leader's waiting for the news!'

The 10 o'clock broadcast was the most carefully produced edition of the news, because it was the one watched by Gaddafi himself. He had his own particular tastes when it came to direction and lighting and his bodyguards would call the television building to demand that the presenter wear specific outfits. Sometimes they would order her to put on the traditional garb of a Libyan bride at the turn of the nineteenth century, at others they would insist that she be a black lady or that her hands be dyed with henna.

And of course it was absolutely forbidden to mention the real names of things on the news. The White House must always be referred to as The Black House, Ronald Reagan as The American Evil and Margaret Thatcher as The Child Murderer. Gaddafi was trying to programme the minds of Libyans with codes to which he alone held the key.

III

The people demand the fall of the Colonel

Mere hours before the start of the revolution in 2011, the very idea of such an uprising was still a joke to be bandied about on Facebook and Twitter. No one believed that Libyans would actually engage in a savage confrontation with Gaddafi, who by this point had attained the status of a bogeyman feared by young and old alike.

Right up until the last moment, Libya's future was examined through the lens of events in Tunisia and Egypt, the underlying question being, 'Will there be a revolution against Gaddafi's regime?' The response was fraught with difficulty. Under Gaddafi all national symbols were done away with, from the national anthem to the flag of independence. This flag, we reckoned, could mean very little to the generations that had grown up in the Colonel's era; their understanding of Libya went no further than an imported anthem and a green flag. We watched revolutionaries in neighbouring Tunisia attack the police stations, only to emerge from their burnt and ravaged shells carrying the very flag that once fluttered over them. We saw Egyptians in Tahrir Square united beneath a single flag, one anthem binding them all.

In Libya the problem was to find a flag to carry. Would Libyans recognize the flag of independence? Were the younger generation even aware that one existed? What could such a flag mean to them now, and if they took to the streets beneath the green banner could that really be considered a revolution against the very man who had created it?

On the night of 15 February, Libya rose up.

Sitting in front of my computer in London I followed events and gave my support on Facebook and Twitter, as did other Libyans living abroad. We wanted to be part this revolution. For my own part, I wanted to be there with them in Benghazi, Tripoli and Misrata, in Nalut and Yafran and all the other towns and cities across the country. I felt for the first time that I belonged to Libya; that I belonged to this land that had drifted away from me and I from it. I sensed the mythical Libyan emerging from his shell: the time had arrived for him to declare that Libya was more than an image of Muammar Gaddafi. Instead of 'The people demand the fall of the regime', the Libyans chanted 'The people demand the fall of the Colonel', and from his military base this same colonel responded by mounting a bloody war against his people, vowing to wipe them out

'inch by inch, block by block, house by house, alley by alley'
– 'zenga, zenga'.

The world witnessed the murderous intent confronting the
Libyan revolutionaries and felt as though they were watching
some fantasy dreamt up in Hollywood. Only Libyans understood the true barbarity of the regime that faced them. They
knew that Libya was no Egypt or Tunisia. They knew that there
was no army to come to their aid because Gaddafi had divided
his armed forces into security militias commanded by his
sons. The world chuckled at Gaddafi's speeches, mocking his
absurdities and cracking jokes, but Libyans stayed silent. They
knew that the speech he delivered from Bab al-Aziziya was
no joke. They'd heard it all before in the 1980s. They'd heard it
hundreds of times over, and this time, they knew, there would
be no hangings, but a genocidal war directed by the Colonel
and his children. Libyans know that Gaddafi's jokes are fatal,
toxic: a wave of crimes beyond human imagining churn in
their wake. Yet now, at least, the world was watching Libya.
The world had discovered Libyans.

Those in the Libyan diaspora began seeing images of Libya
in the local and international press – headlines that talked not
of Gaddafi but of ordinary Libyans. In the newsagents I stood
dazed before the serried ranks of newsprint. On the front
page of every paper, from local freesheets to the international
giants, the word 'Libya' leapt out, followed by pictures of
revolutionaries riding in cars and tanks or waving signs
with messages and slogans denouncing Gaddafi's regime.
Overnight the Libyan had emerged from the isolation in which
Gaddafi had surrounded him for decades. News bulletins led
with Libya. The heroes of the revolution were talking to all the
media outlets, Arab, British, American and French. Gaddafi
had kept Libyans away from the world's television screens
because he couldn't stomach the idea of any well-dressed, well-
spoken Libyan stealing his thunder. The revolution destroyed
not just Gaddafi, but fear and shame and the Libyan instinct
for self-isolation.

When the revolution first started my friend, the Libyan author Giuma Bukleb, said to me: 'For 40 years we've stood afraid and trembling before Gaddafi and now at last we see him standing there trembling.'

It made me laugh hysterically to think of Big Brother shaking and pissing himself with fear.

Giuma Bukleb is one of those who spent a decade in prison for his participation in the student uprising of 1976. He was first thrown out of university, then in 1978 he was rounded up with a large group of intellectuals and writers while attending a literary event in Benghazi. The wave of arrests targeting authors and poets created a yawning chasm in the country's cultural life. An entire generation disappeared, leaving the Libya of the 1980s in the care of the revolutionary committees and the military hacks who were appointed to key government posts and ran the newspapers and publishing houses. The voice of younger generations, and writing itself, vanished, only to resurface in the mid-1990s.

It was around this time in February 2011 that I re-established contact with my childhood friends Khairi, Baaisho and Altakali. Faris had died in a car accident back in 2009.

I spoke to Khairi and asked him how he was doing and it was a joy to hear his voice. He told me that he was going to join the revolution, to sweep away the regime in the company of Baaisho, Altakali and others. I was delighted.

I began to call them constantly asking them how things were going in Tripoli. I heard about the latest chants and slogans, how everyone was saying, 'The people demand the fall of the Colonel'. The Libyan people know that there's no such thing as a political regime in their country. The regime and the government are all Colonel Muammar Gaddafi, and if he does not fall then nothing will.

I called them every day. One moment we would be recalling childhood memories and the next discussing current events. I insisted that I would return to Libya eventually, that we would meet up and make mischief like the old days. They would pass on the latest news and I wrote it up on Twitter or Facebook, or put it in some report.

**

After Eastern Libya had been wrested from his control and Gaddafi's Arab and African mercenaries were deployed around Tripoli, the city's revolutionaries and rebels began to wage a psychological war against the regime. They started by painting stray cats and dogs in the colours of the flag of independence and releasing them to roam the alleyways and streets of residential neighbourhoods. The mercenaries and security services became hunters of animals, shooting the strays and burning their bodies. The revolutionaries then turned to pigeons, painting them up then driving by the State Command Centre, or Gaddafi's residence in Bab al-Aziziya, and releasing them to fly their three-coloured defiance past the Colonel's home.

**

What are these feelings, this blend of joy and sadness, delight and despair, dancing and silence. I found myself at a computer, condemned to eternal unease, to bear my cross on my shoulders as I stride down a road of pain. From here to Tripoli nothing remains of this homeland but news broadcasts and newspaper headlines.

This is what I wrote on the evening of 21 February, the day of sadness, the day the cross of tears was lowered across my back, the day I learnt that my three friends had sacrificed their lives for freedom. I went to a bar in West London, ordered a beer, poured it and sat staring at the empty bottle on the bar top before me. I looked at the papers scattered on the table and listened to the inebriated laughter. I examined my glass of beer and emptied it into myself in one go, then I left. On the way home I felt my pain deep within me. I remembered the old lady. A friend had told me about the time she had asked her grandmother how she was. 'All my friends are dead,' came the reply. 'How do you think I am?'

At some point I started to lose my certainty. I wanted to go to Libya at any price, but before I could travel I had to overcome a number of obstacles. First of all, before I went anywhere, I wanted to get my degree, an MA and a doctorate. I didn't want to return as the Mohamed who spent his time loafing about Tripoli, but as a famous author whose works filled bookshops around the world. I wanted to return with my dreams a reality, my ambitions fulfilled. I wanted to have one up on my relatives who led comfortable lives bankrolled by their parents, and show them that I had made something of myself through my own hard work.

And so it was that I came to a crucial period of my life in London. I had just started the second year of my undergraduate degree after years spent learning the English language and was now assistant manager of an independent bookshop in a fancy West London neighbourhood. If I left for Libya now I would be forced to retake my second year, not to mention losing my job.

Then again, I wanted to go back to see my old friends, friends I haven't seen to this day. I wanted to walk with them through our old haunts in Tripoli; down Omar al-Mukhtar Street with its Egyptian coffee shops where they sell illegal liquor and Viagra, through Zawiyat al-Dahmani, al-Zahara and Haiti, to the Old Town and Casablanca. I wanted to sit with them on hot summer mornings at a cafe in Kennedy Street. But my friends have gone and my Tripoli is another city, a memory splintered by Gaddafi's shells.

IV

In 2004 my mother discovered the internet. She joined forums and websites under an assumed name and soon learned to type. I would watch her writing with pen and paper, typing it up and squirreling the printed sheets away. When I asked her what she was doing she would tell me, 'work'.

She concealed her 'work' even from my father. Truth be told, I wasn't that bothered. My mind was fully occupied with hanging out in the street, playing with my friends, skipping school and the search for true love.

Then one day my mother handed me a floppy disk and a sheet of paper containing an email address, and told me to take them to an internet cafe in al-Zawiya Street (some distance from where we lived in central Tripoli) where I was to send the file on the disk to the address on the paper. She had a wary look about her as she handed the disk over. I was not to open the file, or read it, or show it to anyone, or take anyone along with me. I was to open a new email account in a false name and be careful not to leave the disk in the machine when I was finished. I protested. Our street was full of internet cafes, I told her. We had a connection in the house. Why did I have to go all the way to al-Zawiya Street?

She held out three dinars and asked me to keep my mouth shut and obey her. Sighing loudly I took the disk and the piece of paper and left the house, walking for nearly an hour until I came to al-Zawiya Street. I sat down next to an old man browsing through porn sites and fondling his penis, and I inserted the disk into the computer.

I decided to take a look at what was on it.

An untitled Word file. I double clicked and waited for it to open.

The first line came as a physical shock; I gasped, then closed the file.

This is how Gaddafi and his men govern us.

I opened a browser window, typed 'sex' into Google and looked at porn sites for an hour. Then I went home.

My mother asked me if I had sent the file and I told her no; the internet had been too slow to upload a file into an email.

She shook her head and asked me for the floppy disk. My hand went into my pocket and searched around. It wasn't there. I told her and she slapped her cheeks, then slapped me and started to scream in my face, 'I've had it! It's over, I've been discovered!'

She began to beat herself.

When I said that I would go and fetch it, she grabbed my shirt.

'Swear on your life that you'll never go there again. Never. It's not safe any more.'

I can't explain what instinct made me abandon the disk like that, after plunging myself into the oblivion of that everyday activity, browsing porn. Needless to say, I never went back.

But my mother did not stop there. From time to time she would ask me to send a file for her from a new email account and I became something of an expert at this game. I would go to some distant neighbourhood, select an internet cafe at random and sit at a computer out of sight of the manager and his customers. When the manager got up from the computer screen where he monitored and controlled the other machines, I would quickly set up an account and send the file then having removed the disk and paid for my time I would leave the place, never to return.

That is, until my father found out. It was actually my mother who told him about her political activities; she was unable to keep it from him for long. At first my father became very agitated, refusing to talk to either of us, and from time to time throughout the day I heard raised voices.

That evening my mother was still trying to soothe him, but my father could think of nothing but the consequences of my mother being found out: the family would break up; we might never see her again.

Another day: we were all in the car together, my brother, my sister and I in the back, my father driving and my mother alongside him. To our left ran the coastal road, to our right, the ancient walls of the Old Town. My father stopped the car.

He got out and stood gazing at the sea, while my mother, her eyes fixed on the town walls placed her hand to her cheek. My siblings and I were bickering from sheer boredom and my brother called out to our father to come and settle the dispute.

'Shut your mouth,' my father told him.

We fell silent and stared at each other for a while, then at our mother. We twisted round and saw our father, his back turned to us, still watching the sea.

A few days later we were all on an aeroplane. Landing at Manchester airport we were met by a friend of my father's and taken to a small, furnished house. In Manchester, my mother found the freedom she needed to write, and she started working for Libya's opposition press.

V

At the beginning of the revolution my contacts with friends and family in Libya made me an important source of information about the latest developments there. People started following my Twitter posts and I set up a Facebook page in support of the revolution where I posted articles and video clips. For three whole days I didn't sleep. I kept it up until the shock of my friends' deaths left me paralysed, incapable of writing or monitoring the news. I spent my days working at the bookshop, and in the evenings, abandoning my studies, I went out to drink beer and smoke hash with friends for whom Libya was no more than a name in their daily paper.

When NATO intervened in the revolution I punched the air, clapped and celebrated. Many Arabs were dead set against the idea, which they saw as marking the end of the Arab Spring. They opposed it vociferously: Libya would be the ruin of the Arab revolution. But Libyans knew that NATO was no saviour alighting from the distant heavens. Rejecting the idea of a Western land campaign they stood ready to oppose any attempt to stage a landing, but were powerless to prevent the imposition of a no-fly zone. I had many an argument over this point with my friends from Palestine, Egypt and Syria. They claimed that Arab countries would help Libya in place of Europe and America – a truly laughable proposition. Gaddafi had funded a whole host of African insurgencies and had at his disposal an army of mercenaries. Sudan's rebel movements, for instance, had been financed by the Colonel purely so they would fight on his side and armed convoys were making their way towards Benghazi to wipe it out 'inch by inch, block by block, house by house, alley by alley'. We needed NATO's intervention and the air blockade to prevent a humanitarian catastrophe overtaking the people being bombarded by Gaddafi's Tripoli-based air force, to ward off the convoys of heavily armed mercenaries heading to Benghazi with the aim of turning it into the world's biggest graveyard. When my friends – friends no longer – asked me why NATO hadn't intervened in Yemen or Syria, for example, my answer was clear: Gaddafi has enough wealth, evil and insanity to kill the entire Libyan people. He could quite easily turn Libya into a 'fiery hell', as he himself said in one of his speeches. We took to the streets in peaceful demonstrations and our skulls and chests were ripped apart by anti-aircraft rounds. We saw Grad rockets level the homes of civilians, we saw children exterminated in the street, and when the revolutionaries took up arms, when we allowed NATO to intervene, this was merely a furtherance of a vow that was constantly on the lips of the revolutionaries themselves: 'The blood of the martyrs shall not be spilt in vain.'

Most of the revolutionaries carrying weapons have never used a gun in anger; they might have learnt a little in Gaddafi's militarized high schools, but they are essentially novices at war.

And the same goes for me. Because I attended high school in Tripoli I was taught to strip, reassemble and load a Kalashnikov. One of the revolutionaries said that the only thing the Libyan people should thank Gaddafi for was forcing them to learn about guns. True, the Colonel had intended the young scholars to become 'the leader's bodyguard' but he made it possible for them to prosecute a war against him.

My mother continued to write about what was going on. She turned up on television and phone-ins and was mentioned by Gaddafi's broadcasters, who referred to her as the 'whore' and the agent of the Americans and Zionists. Her brothers were led off to the secret police headquarters in Tripoli and questioned about their correspondence with her. Their daughters stopped leaving the house, fearful of abduction. Our family was now a clan of 'rats', to use Gaddafi's phrase.

For his part my father donated what money he could, kept in touch with his family and tried to keep abreast of the latest developments. Sometimes a man reaches a point when he has to see things for himself. My father wanted to go to Libya to be with the revolutionaries. A wife and children are obstacles that have stopped many Libyans returning home.

At the height of the Libyan uprising in early April 2011 I told myself: I don't belong here. I can't stay here. My place is over there, in Libya, where a revolution is rising up like a phoenix. I've prayed for it, I've dreamt of it, I felt that it would never come. I belong in the ranks of the men fighting on the front lines of the war against the tyrant and his mercenaries.

It was only then that I felt able to lay my head on Libya's bosom and confess my sin.

This story doesn't end here. The truth is that there are many stories that need to be told. The Libyan revolution will not end when Gaddafi is finished; there will be many challenges in the way of a people who have never known the meaning of democracy or been accustomed to the workings of a functioning government. And then there are all those stories that I should really have set down here: of the communists in the seventies, of the intellectuals in the fifties and sixties who dreamed of establishing a true Libyan nation state, of the men killed by Gaddafi in the Abu Slim prison in the mid-seventies and the decade-long international embargo on the country. This is a people that have borne the weight of enough stories to fill all the novels and films you could wish for. To be continued ...

London
May 2011

4

WE ARE NOT SWALLOWS (ALGERIA)

By Ghania Mouffok
Translated from the French by Georgina Collins

'Soon "they" are going to put metres round our necks and measure the air we breathe and charge us for it,' a young man said to me.

Don't interrupt me. Don't ask me who 'they' are. Because it's 'them' too. 'They', 'them' – that's what we call our indescribable leaders. That's how we keep them at a distance from our destinies, our descendants. They bring bad luck and we know that. Don't interrupt me. I'm writing so I don't forget. Otherwise soon I'll forget. It was winter 2011, the day after rioting. It was just before the spring, or just after. I don't know any more, but it was before Arabs became celebrities and celebrated. We were on a street corner in Algiers, not far from Cervantes' cave, named after the author of *Don Quixote* who was reduced to slavery by our ancestors and lay hidden in the cave, watching the sea through holes in the limestone rocks, waiting for freedom.

We were in one of those so-called *quartiers populaires* of Algiers. That's what we call the neighbourhoods with creaking windows and buckling walls upon which you can build the memory of a country. These districts are neither old enough to deserve a museum nor young enough to stink of tedium, the kind of place you can get yourself a proper coffee, you know, still a whole *commedia dell'arte*, without the inflated price-tag of a Columbian espresso. I'd come to ask this young man why he's angry. 'Why are you setting your neighbourhood on fire? Why are you scaring your mother and the bourgeoisie?'

'I'm like a volcano,' he said. 'It's so I can breathe.'

He wasn't angry, actually. He was really very calm. His eyes scanned the street which had now been cleared of any sign of fire, whilst his body still held the smell of riots, this mixture of powder and vinegar: powder from the tear gas grenades, vinegar for the eyes (otherwise they cry, the eyes of rioters).

He was happy.

'The good thing about rioting,' he said, 'is that afterwards they come and collect the rubbish. Usually they forget about it and it doesn't smell very nice.' He dragged on a cigarette like only 20-year-old kids know how: with pleasure and conviction, his fingers still white. But he was under house arrest, bound to his little patch of the neighbourhood, to his little street.

'After rioting,' he said, 'you have to stay put. You have to cast anchor into the tarmac of your neighbourhood, stay close to home and wait, otherwise they'll catch you like fish. Can't you see their wire nets?' he asked me. 'Look, they're spread over every exit from the neighbourhood. And if you're unlucky enough to get close to the fishermen in boots and helmets, that's it, you're done for. Before you've even understood what's happening to you, you're caught up with their haul and on the way to prison. In the courts, the bounty hunters will cite "public order offence", or "criminal damage" and in place of freedom, they put you in a cage for eternity and a day, while your mother, a little more pale than usual, does the rounds of all the prisons, taking a box of cakes and a packet of tissues as gifts. They treat us like fish in an aquarium they are slowly draining of water,' the young man said.

On the other side of the world, people said we're Arabs, that it's the Arab Spring, but it was winter.

In Algeria, swallows come in spring, but we're not swallows. We're Arabs, but first and foremost we're ourselves. When we rise up like waves, we win back our bodies, rediscover our spirits and answer only to ourselves. That's what that young man taught me, the one who spoke like a poet about breathing.

We were in one of those districts – a *quartier populaire* – where every generation passes on, if not history, from father to son, at least a glance, a smirk, a look from one father to another. It happens behind the walls, beyond the Kasbah where the lives of fathers and sons are piled on top of one another, sharing the same mattresses, the same old pots and pans.

The spring lasts a season, while our path will be long, as long as those baboons reign over us, stealing our time, plundering our part of the world. Like greedy, indifferent snakes, they wind barbed wire around both our bodies and our spirits. In any case, that's what the young man calls the cops of our dictatorship, the young man who still smells of riots. He calls them 'snakes'. They live amongst us, and you might think their venom is weak, but it's noxious. 'They poison us,' the young man said.

So one day he rises up. Why that day? I don't know. And he takes some stones and matches and sets fire to the invisible walls of his neighbourhood. And beneath his own windows he creates a Sioux fire.

The *petit-bourgeois*, as we used to call them, look through their windows at the smoke drifting through the sky and say: 'Why are they destroying their own neighbourhoods? They don't have to wreck the place. Oh no! Look! Look, Belcourt is on fire! What a nightmare … and they don't even have any demands!'

'But, dear lady,' the young man said to me, 'we demand to breathe, and that's a big enough demand in itself.' Through fire and violence, that demand opens up a breathing space, it pushes back the walls of snakes to the borders of the district, and it restores freedom to both night and day. Well, to some nights and some days. And suddenly, the intoxication of time passing by belongs to you.

'Rioting is a way of breathing,' the young man said to me. 'Tell them we won't make excuses for living.' We laughed and I left. But he stayed: 'like a caged bird, flying round in circles,' he said. As for me, I left like a thief with these gems:

We are not swallows. We're not just making spring but also winter, autumn and summer too, because we've been around for a long time.

And I left.

I'm a witness, a female witness, a lonely witness to these many voices. I take to the streets, take flight, take a look at all this anger, and I like doing that. I like to gather up all that anger when it first takes the pathway of dissent. I prefer it without violence, but always with courage, when it cries out without destroying hope, and when it says: 'see you tomorrow'.

This is how I gather words. I take my harvest back to the house, sometimes scrawled on a scrap of crumpled paper when I've unexpectedly run into people protesting as I go about my daily life. Sometimes I write in an exercise book. And in the margins, I inscribe the telephone numbers of people I still don't know, even though I always say to them: 'see you tomorrow'.

Sometimes I take my son, all of nine years old, along to watch the protests, like you'd take your child to a museum. And I say to him: 'Look! They're angry and they have reason to be.' His wide eyes watch the cops and he says '*démocratiya*' to them in Arabic. Despite this, when I ask him what he's going to be when he grows up, he says 'a police officer'. His world, mine, ours is full of cops, barricades, sirens, the echoes of closing doors that impregnate our memories with their power. The cops are these robocops dressed in blue, with helmets, boots and riot shields that are see-through close up, and they have heavy wooden batons that can crush your skull. I'm not naive, I'm over 50 and I know that the destinies of men and women are likely to be unpredictable, probably improbable. And while I lead my son down the paths of protest like this, it's not to teach him anything, but just to show him that being a citizen of Algeria can be joyous, chaotic and rebellious.

So, with a lesson of my own, I offset the *tarbiya madaniya*, a strange subject that's taught at primary school in Algeria. It's sort of a lesson in public conduct where they teach children obedience under the pretext of 'living in harmony'. The textbook for this subject is ugly, and it's also an accurate guide to what is forbidden. The word 'freedom' is banned from its pages. That's how childhood is approached in Algeria.

In place of literature, and in the language of Mahmoud Darwish,* my son learns to recite an absurd text that praises the police. My child is in the third year of mainstream primary school in Algeria. In the evening when we're revising for the following day by going through his school books, together we learn how our leaders construct their ideal citizen. Love for country is confused with love for the authority established by them. Under the trees in the playground, children stand to attention and sing the national anthem as the flag is raised. As a form of amusement, once again they're taught how to draw our national symbol in green and red, with the crescent moon and star, so they'll start dreaming about it from the age of six.

'Nationalism against terrorism.' That's the response given by our leaders with the steel helmets and paper dollars. They've invented the phrase to teach younger generations the sacrifices of their elders – whose history was stolen, memories hacked away by the strokes of a sickle.

This epic has gone on 130 years, but they only like to remember the eight year 'war of national liberation' from 1954 to 1962: the date of Algerian independence. And from that period, they only like to remember the word 'war'. It was an

---

* Mahmoud Darwish was an iconic Palestinian poet and author (1941–2008).

incredible denial of colonial order, oppression and exploitation, a movement that was fed by a demand for freedom, equality, justice, by Vietnam, workers' struggles and debates cultivated by ideas, by all these intangible outbursts that nourished the stories of our past, and it's been reduced, squeezed into hideous history books, or into a statue of a third world robocop erected in our town squares and public gardens. Here's to the weapons! Here's to the boots and helmets that liberated our country while gravestones crushed the faces of our heroes. Forget Abane Ramdane's* words of April 1957: 'We will save our liberty come hell or high water. Even if in doing so we leave behind our skin.'

And so it was. Some months later he left his skin in the hands of his jailers, the brothers in arms who assassinated him, strangled him, consumed by their great ambition and madness, possessed by a taste for power. They'd become snakes already … As for freedom, we'll have to wait.

Abane Ramdane is dead, he was assassinated, strangled by his own people, my own people, while the tortured body of Algeria along with its impoverished population was completely unaware; too busy chasing away France which was refusing to let go of our country. France wanted to keep it all for itself, along with the taste of the vine, matured in the sun and nourished by the hunger of the indigenous people. Lies and propaganda. Abane Ramdane – did he not die in combat?

In 1962, Jean-Paul Sartre** said: 'Today no one is unaware that we have ruined, starved and massacred a nation of poor people to bring them to their knees. They remained standing. But at what price!' (Sartre 2001, *Colonialism and Neo-Colonialism*, Routledge, p.72).

We've paid a heavy price.

---

* Abane Ramdane, a key figure in the movement for Algerian independence, was assassinated in 1957.

** Jean-Paul Sartre (1905–1980) was a French philosopher and notable supporter of Algerian independence.

The number of corpses in our 'Republic of lies' piles up, but our memories rebel. That's what happens. Can our memories do otherwise, I wonder? Sometimes I write; sometimes I've had enough – that's the truth. It's my head that rebels, weary of writing the same old story, the story of all this miserable conflict and resistance. I remember the riots in Kabylie; I forget what year it was. But I remember I was hot, it was hot and it was like they had been suckled on bitterness from the baby's bottle. I remember these youths acting like Hercules as they pulled the park fencing from the ground, reducing it to ashes before I'd even managed to find a corner in the shade where I could sweat. Fury had increased their strength tenfold, I remember. And I remember the rotten feet of this old man searching for his son, who's still searching for him, missing in action like a cloud, disappeared.

'They turned him to dust,' he told me. But I remember his feet and how the ground formed a sort of second skin around them like that of a Mitidja farmer. And I remember his sad eyes; how could I forget. His eyes held an absolute sadness, and the hope that I'd take down his story, when all I really gave a damn about were 'the mothers of the missing'.

It's true: these women fascinated me. While I was hiding in fear, they'd uncovered a hidden geography, a new map of the place. They'd learned the way to the barracks where their children, sons, husbands, had been swallowed up, seized by night, and by day too, and who'd been missing ever since. They knew that time was more precious than their lives. They're still searching today. For some, their courage seems unbearable. Others, they say: 'It's over, time to forget.'

But I remember the earth around that old man's feet. The man whose eyes held an absolute sadness. I remember the night, still carefree, when I met a battalion of red berets for the first time. It was like being in Gillo Pontecorvo's film *The Battle of Algiers*. They were advancing down my street like foreign troops, and I think they were carrying bayonets. Yes, bayonets. Yes, they were paras, like in *The Battle of Algiers*, and it was happening right near my home. I remember it was 1988. Five hundred people died in the streets where I live. They fell to the ground like overripe fruit, a spoiled trajectory.

I remember this field of broad beans, flowering around the ruins at Tipaza. Geraniums sprang from old pots in windows; blood stained the ground where people had been massacred in the night. Women and children took refuge in their rural homes, and they made shields from corn leaves and reeds, but those shields were unable to protect them from death. Death by their own tools, tools they'd sweated and toiled with. Lying beside them were the pickaxes, billhooks, shovels that had surprised them in the night. Death at the hands of the unknown, called 'terrorists', for want of a better word. They came as they left – on foot – carrying away the pubescent girls whose father, in his misfortune, survived. Powerless, he'd hidden behind the reeds, witnessing the death throes of his own life. With calloused hands, he'd gathered up the identity cards that belonged to his decimated family, and he showed them to me as a kind of proof that these people had at one time been living there. I don't know, I remember those pots of geraniums at the windows, overlooking the pathway of death. Why here? In my home? In our home? Why are horror and the magnificence of the *maquis* always so entwined?

I remember this kid spying on me from across the car park in a large doorway while I was doing my usual shopping for the evening as it drew in around me. He was spying on me and, like an idiot, I no longer knew whether to shout for help because he wanted to kill me, or whether I'd look stupid because maybe he just wanted to talk to me and tell me I was beautiful. I remember his eyes; I think he was frightened. I was too.

I remember I ran away. I escaped death in a car park. I took my prayer mat and I left. Yes, I fled. In a country of strangers, I was given a microphone and I spoke. They said I was a witness, a precious spectator. 'But then where are the actors?' I said. And so I returned, I returned to my country. But no one was waiting for me. I'm not complaining: there were 200,000 dead to bury.

I remember their blood spattered over every TV screen on the planet.

And those of you who talk about the Arab Spring, have you forgotten?

And now, after a civil war of 30 years, a hundred years, as though in a Greek tragedy we're forbidden from talking about our misfortune. 'It's over,' they said. 'There's peace now. Peace.'

To go through all that for this! Today we're not allowed to protest. What am I saying? We're not allowed to walk down our streets together. State of emergency. State of siege. Whose emergency? What siege? Emergency for 'them', a siege for those of us whose lives are besieged. You know, in my country, we no longer ask each other: 'Are you going on the demonstration tomorrow?' We say 'are you going on the *march* tomorrow?'

'Marching' has become a synonym for protesting. Maybe because at least marching means you have to stand, when 'they' have condemned us to be slugs, merely creeping along the ground.

And yet we march. We march through every town across the country.

We march against the riot shields and grenades, the rows of cops both in uniform and plain clothes, and we march against the cops that control our minds as well. We march, a centimetre here and a centimetre there. We advance, we draw back, standing up on our own two feet. The cops no longer shoot at us – that's true. We're no longer rabbits since the West taught our tyrants the art of what they call 'conflict management'. When you're suppressing people, you don't shoot them at point blank range, you have to be reasonable instead and use the reasonable weapons the West supplies you with: batons as big as tree trunks, gleaming 4x4s, motorbikes, sunglasses, leather boots, transparent shields, walkie-talkies, apache helicopters, highly visible cameras that spy on us in our neighbourhoods, etc ... etc ... Tear gas grenades – no longer 'point blank', but a weapon in the air.

Sometimes, alongside others, I march from the pavement to the street, advancing just a few centimetres whilst the new 'gentle' cops push us back, like a living bulldozer. Sometimes we even stop the traffic for a few moments: we're delighted and we congratulate each other. Tomorrow the headline will be: 'they marched'. And the next day we'll have to start again, just like Sisyphus carrying his rock.

My Tunisian friend said: 'What are you Algerians waiting for?'

And I didn't reply. Instead, I complimented him. '*Mabrouk alef mabrouk,*' I said to him stupidly, 'Congratulations,' as if he was celebrating his marriage. '*Yau, yau, yau!*' I don't have the words to accommodate political victories.

'How did you do it?' I said to him. 'What's your secret?'

'Honestly ...' he replied. It was over the telephone so I couldn't see his face. 'Honestly,' he replied, 'I don't know. I followed the youth,' said he, who'd been fighting for so long.

I cried, I told him, I don't know how to celebrate this surreal kind of achievement. These days it's not the fighting, but the victory that's revolutionary on Arab soil. I told him that one day, just for one day before I die, I'd like to be that young man in the town square, alone, in the light of a street lamp, captured in time on a mobile phone, crying out with joy: '*Al-sha'b al-tunisi hurr.*' 'We're free tonight!' Our Mafioso-style dictator has left; the bastard ran away!

Then from Tahrir Square, we heard a battle cry: '*Al-sha'b yurid isqat al-nizam.*' 'The people demand the fall of the regime.' And the Egyptians were granted their wish: they'd won. Two out of two. And my Egyptian friend said: 'What are you Algerians waiting for?'

I said nothing, it was over the telephone. Instead, I said: '*Alef mabrouk, yau, yau, yau,*' as if I was congratulating her on her marriage. I don't have the words in Arabic to celebrate political victories.

They say we're making spring, but we're not swallows. The Arabs are waking up, they said. But were they sleeping like peaceful little mice whose fields were destroyed long ago? Maybe it's you people in the West who are finally writing us back into history, the history of the world we've been excluded from, hidden from because it's well known that 'Arabs' believe in fate, in *Mektoub*. They pray under canvas while they wait for paradise. *Allahu Akbar*.

In Syria, I saw women singing the national anthem. It was a day of rest, yes I was resting, tired, depressed – life's a bitch. I was in my lounge when they came on TV. It was like they'd broken in.

They were neither laughing nor crying. They were singing in chorus for Hamza, who'd been killed. They'd come together, creating this picture in my little room. And they were protesting in their room by singing the national anthem. Neither laughing nor crying, but standing, singing in chorus. They all had their faces hidden, but God they were beautiful, standing up straight like that. Now, here in my lounge with their candles burning on my table, they took me by the hand, pulled me up, and with them, finally, I was able to cry. I cry for the body of the martyred child, Hamza al-Khatib, son of the town of Deraa, killed, assassinated, emasculated. He was 13 years old. It was just after the Arab Spring.

The following day, I saw Hillary Clinton on the television. Unperturbed, she said: 'I can only hope that this child did not die in vain.' She had the same old blonde hair, hair that had never encountered strong winds, or maybe she had banned it from moving.

I said to her: 'Let go of my hand, you fool. Your hair smells of oil and grief.'

I might make fun of Clinton, but I don't like it when she makes fun of me, when she claims she wants to 'liberate' me. Just like she's liberated the Iraqis, Afghans and Palestinians, fettered to her veto like a black slave to his chains. Like she's just liberated Libya? Yes, I know bloated Gaddafi's gone. But what's happened to the Libyans? I'm missing a picture of 'liberated' Libya. I'm missing the Libyans, my neighbours. A sound is missing. I didn't hear the Libyans shout out '*al-sha'b yurid*', the people demand. That clear, ripe phrase. Its obvious simplicity signals revolution like dawn signals day. Sovereignty without a kingdom: the people demand.

And what does NATO want? To save the Libyans from their dictator? What a tasteless joke.

I'm also missing something else from Libya – the face of NATO as it flies, swims, runs along our borders, across the sea and throughout the land. Why is it quietly keeping out of sight? What do the coalition forces look like? What can you see on the faces of those poor soldiers when again they embark on a war that's not their own?

In Algiers I met a cameraman. We drank tea together. He was returning from Libya, from the land of insurgents. He admitted he'd spotted NATO soldiers masquerading as Libyans. These men were directing surgical strikes from the ground, and he told me they were incredibly precise, and there was no doubt it was completely different to the old-style colonial butchery.

The cameraman, a little perplexed, added that now and then he saw a bunch of Rambos disguised as Libyans, and it was funny the way he described them. He said they had pecs like elephants and wore vests that were too small to contain them. They had boots like proper warriors, while the Libyans were fighting the war in their sandals. Now and then he saw them go nuts. They were desperate because the Libyan insurgents lacked discipline and they were trying to turn them into soldiers. He said the lack of discipline took nothing away from their courage, but that he most definitely needed his ten-ton bulletproof vest, even in the desert when he was kilometres from the fighting. He needed it because the insurgents seemed confused handling their brand new weapons, and now and then one of the Rambos had to come and explain that a gun isn't a toy and that it's held like this, with the barrel at the bottom. And it's not an arm extension that you use to point out where the fighting is, or to scratch your ear. And I'm not making any of that up.

Where are the Libyans? They've been deprived of their Spring, and from now on they're divided into good and bad Libyans. They're all witnesses now to an odyssey in which they no longer play just minor roles. My memory of the world now reminds me: the enemies of my enemies are not my friends. I wouldn't like someone to come and save me by bombing my town, I wouldn't like that at all. The same as I don't like knowing that American drones are flying around the Mediterranean between Corsica and Tripoli, ready for who knows what war. Are they the same as those used in Iraq, Pakistan and Afghanistan? And what was Obama doing at that time? He tried to do the samba in Brazil and play football in the favelas, while the world's eyes lingered on Michelle in her ballet pumps, beating time – irresistible. When the president of the largest world power turns his back on a 'humanitarian operation' that he's been actively involved in, you have to watch out. What's he refusing to look at? And what can we veil our faces with so we don't see this rescue attempt that only reminds us of Europe's colonial 'civilizing missions'. No, the enemies of my enemies are definitely not my friends. On television tomorrow, who'll remember that some 'tribes' paid the price in blood?

So what are the Algerians waiting for? They're not waiting, they don't have time. They're on time according to their clock, which tells them it's time to learn to walk together, as a group, by occupation, by organization, as sculptors of this ongoing revolution. After the civil war, the Algerians found themselves another war: the cold war against the criminals who've taken over as their leaders. I harass you, you harass me. What more do you want? We've created a spectacular civil war, full of blood and sacrifice. We killed a president in Annaba – Mohamed Boudiaf –

and the assassin is in our jails, with his steely gaze. They say he's a soldier. We've changed government ten times, twenty times, a hundred times, as many times as the seasons have changed.

And we've sentenced each government to prison behind their own four walls. That's how much we hate them. They're banned from our districts and they've transformed their own into bunkers. Like Judas, they watch us from peepholes in their doors, while we send them clear signs of hatred. Time and time again, they are forced to erect barriers around themselves whilst they pillage us. All this we know.

They became twice as vicious, so the strongest of us met up at night, constructed small makeshift boats and took to the sea with a water drum and a petrol can. We abandoned our bodies to the sea so we could get to know the kingfish. You see survivors on TV on the other side of the ocean, being welcomed by men and women who put on fresh gloves before giving out stale bread. Others choose to set fire to themselves. There's no point discussing it. You imagine what it means to sacrifice yourself. One morning, I imagine, you get up, leave your little house, take some change, cross the street and go to the petrol station. And what do you say: 'Give me a few litres of that shitty petrol that's all the rage, because I want to set myself on fire,' before paying, crossing back over the street, and checking out the place where you're going to make a spectacle of your misery. Before drenching your body with shitty petrol, while the bastards whet their appetites with 100-year-old whisky, before you take the matches, unless it was a lighter, and you flare up, like a Hassi-Messaoud* inferno. It's people who don't know about this who say: 'What are the Algerians waiting for?'

An architect friend said to me: 'Where we live, children die for a scrap of lawn, a swing.'

Every day I wonder: 'How do they find the strength to get up? Where do they get that relentless energy from, energy that

---

* The town of Hassi-Messaoud is at the centre of Algerian oil production.

transforms a thousand-year-old burden into a reed barricade that the wind tears down. And yet they rebuild it again in the morning, with fire in their bellies.'

We bear the burden of contempt, pillage and rape. In Algeria, we carry that misfortune, forever trapped between a vast ocean and a desert full of oil.

Every generation creates a new landscape of the world it plunders like the barons of times gone by. It was the sailors themselves not the thieves who took the share of the booty as they rode upon the waves of history. We travel from land to land, from wave to wave, just like them. They talk about us with compassion, saying: 'Algeria is rich, but the Algerians are poor.'

But that's not it. We're not hungry. Well, not as hungry as we used to be. My mother was born in the twenties and since childhood she'd always had a taste for figs, stolen in a time of typhus and misery. Algeria is the primary importer of durum wheat, and it pays for it in dollars. The bread is thrown out onto the streets where the rats, cats and dogs piss: the ones that rummage through our dustbins. So, we're not hungry, that's not it. But each time we rest, we turn away, we drop our guard, and stop watching from the mountains of our homes, the prisons that are our houses ... the moment we stop, the rotten bastards who prowl around our neighbourhood steal away our taste for bread. And humiliated, we lose the taste of living together. The 'Other' becomes despicable to us and we despise him as much as we despise ourselves. 'Let his mother cry, rather than mine,' we say.

But when his mother cries, we cry harder than he does, guilt gnawing away at us, refusing to be stripped of our humanity. It's not bread these tyrants seek to take from us. Since Spartacus, they've known that slaves must be fed along with the beasts of burden. Every day, with a carrot in their hand and a baton by their side, they draw humanity out of us whilst they binge like geese on borrowed time. I'm sick of you bastards.

Irhal. Leave! You treat this country like a slut: destroying what we create and vandalizing our history. What achievements can you be proud of? Achievements: that's what you call the three bridges you left as a legacy to this country, and we're sick of you. And on TV, when you show images of the time we spat in your face, are you proud?

You've made a hash of the Arab language, a mess of the Berber language, the language of our ancestors. You've reduced our fields of orange trees to cement, our music to folklore and our religion to *fitna* – a source of division amongst people. You made filthy money from our oil, you made a prison of our towns, and a *maquis* of our mountains. Your gaze is as elusive as the flash cars which transport you, like mobile tombs, down our streets; no one admires you but you still flash your lights.

They tell us we are making spring. But you say we're making war. A Tunisian friend said to me: 'They treat us like dogs and then they're surprised when we turn into wolves.'

Wolves. Yes, he's right; we kill each other sometimes. Like fools, we piss where we eat, waiting for permission to live just like the men and women in their country. But it's easy isn't it? A house, roof, job, pavement to walk down, marriage, children. It's so simple.

The TV? We turn the sound off, but sometimes the picture is useful as a nightlight. Maybe in another galaxy, there are little men watching Bouteflika, Ouyahia, the generals in helmets and the invisible ones who pull the strings. And maybe those little men are munching stones and cracking up with laughter. But we're not laughing any more, since the dead no longer rise and it never says 'the end' on our TV screens. They don't make us laugh, nor do they scare us, they poison our lives and we poison theirs, aside from their many dogsbodies who relish the leftovers and act as informers when we've nothing left to hide.

Even though we play hide-and-seek and together we invented dictatorship and anarchy, or should we call it the anarchy of dictatorship, they're shut away in their districts, watching us on screen while their helicopters circle the sky. And we try to walk on the land they reduced to ashes, and in our districts we do as we say, what we want, as we can. The State is me, it's you, we fill the void because it's all they've been capable of creating. Under their windows we've installed an army of age-old free-riders, salesmen on the sly who steal little bits of pavement. And to survive they'll sell any old thing made in China: fake batteries, fake Lacoste and even fake *dinars*. Like a family of clowns the government says: it's forbidden.

'It's forbidden to be so stupid,' the street replied, sniggering. 'Come on and make me obey your laws.' So, they send out the cops to sweep the pavements whilst the street makes a run for it and starts up again somewhere else. The next day, they forget this ludicrous endeavour. Sometimes there are people who steal small bits of wasteland, and while this land is hardly attractive, they make a place to live out of bits and pieces like sheet metal and bricks. Again, they say it's forbidden. So, life's free-riders cock a deaf ear, but they're on the lookout. At night, the bulldozers and cops arrive. The cops again. OK, you want war? You'll have riots. The ashes are still smouldering when they steal the next piece of land. And it all starts again with bits and pieces, and our new district of bricks and sheet metal is born. We drive on the left, on the right, without helmets or licences in our towns peppered with uniforms who look elsewhere because they're tired as well. Algeria is Mad Max, torn between the Qur'an and free-flowing beer. Even the CIA doesn't understand a thing. Tell me, who's in charge of Algeria, this tired country, tired, exhausted and exhausting? I swear no one knows anything about it, anything at all.

So, each generation creates its own battle cry as it waits upon the ruins of the world.

They tell us we are making spring. You say we're making war. With blood and tears rather than jasmine.

When I float through the demonstrations, I like the way today's youth uses the national anthem for a shield, in a happy, ideological, gender fusion in which the hijab meets Che

Guevara. It's a derisory shield against the army of cops that forbids them from moving; and what powerful irony. They've turned our nation's song into a battle cry, when they should be standing to attention. You wanted them to be nationalist and under your thumb, but they've taken things into their own hands.

These young people know nothing about war, despite growing up in the shadow of the last one. And I'm so surprised when I realize I'm old enough to be their mother. Sometimes they call me *tata*, and lo and behold I suddenly realize that I've aged. They're not like me; they're entering an era that I'll leave behind. I come from a time gone by which was filled with melancholy. What is lost is lost.

Their feet are firmly planted on the ground whilst my head was in the clouds, in the euphoria of constructing a new country, going from a paper revolution to a cardboard one. I've already lived between two wars, one of liberation, the other of destruction. I'm the same age as Algeria. And, in the shadow of tanks, I did not revolt. I'm the same age as a country that's taught me patience and modesty. Who am I to ask them to do what I couldn't?

And as time flies by, why aren't you Westerners outraged by the dictatorship of your 'volatile' markets?

And you, the reader … whether you're white, black or red, man or woman, from the East or West, do you know that my prison is yours and your freedom will be mine? They said we're making spring. But you, reader … do you know that we're not swallows? We're the people of the world.

Algiers
October 2011

5

THE RESISTANCE

ARMED WITH WORDS (YEMEN)

By Jamal Jubran
Translated from the Arabic by Robin Moger

I

I look back now at the life I've led, at my childhood, and ask myself: How is it that I experienced such pain?

I was a singularly ungifted child, physically weak and always afraid of others, something that stemmed from the fact I was born outside of Yemen, where I came with my family when I was not even a year and a half old. My father had decided to leave Eritrea and return to Yemen, his homeland, after long years of exile and so my Eritrean mother, unwilling to be parted from those she loved, was forced to abandon her country and come with us.

We returned.

We had nothing. My father had to start his life again from scratch. It is impossible to convey how poor we were, living together in a single room.

My brothers all spoke excellent Arabic, acquired at the only school in Asmara that offered the children of Arab exiles an education in their mother tongue. I never got the chance, which was only natural, since I was still breastfeeding at the time, my talents confined to crying and nestling in my mother's arms.

Slowly, painfully, I grew up. Useless at everything, unable to pronounce a single intelligible sentence in Arabic, I failed to get into school when I was old enough to go. My stock response, when approached by Yemenis or asked to do anything, was to weep. I was scared of strangers, which meant I had to stay close to a family member at all times. The task of looking after me was divided between my mother and my siblings according to the time they could spare. It was out of the question to leave me alone to face the cruelty of the world around me, a world I could not negotiate with words. The neighbourhood kids, for instance, would beat me up for the slightest reason, or for none, exploiting my inability to express myself in Arabic and my puny physique.

Then something happened that turned my life upside down and changed everything.

One day, with my seventh birthday in sight, I went to the cinema for the first time in my life and there I discovered the world as I wanted it to be, a world that compensated me for a reality in which I was yet to find my place.

It was an Indian film. I watched the hero defeat swarms of enemies with a single blow, a victory, it seemed, that was out of my reach. Now I knew how to get to the cinema on my own – it wasn't far from where we lived – I was there every day. It became my own alternative universe, a place where I could slip into the guise of the one-punch hero and take revenge on the world, on the little bastards from the alley who took turns to beat me whenever they found me alone and unprotected.

What could be more delightful than laying low armies of your foes with a single swing of the fist?

Cinema gave me a certain inner steel and I managed to get into school by uttering a few Arabic phrases I had picked up by mixing with people at my beloved picture house. Now a student, my regular attendance at the cinema began to drop off and as my school career progressed, the visual imagination of film was replaced with words. I was dazzled by a new discovery: the alchemy of letters rearranged to form illimitable strings of words and convey innumerable meanings. I was a newcomer to the Arabic language, a beginner taking his first steps, but it was already clear that my relationship with these letters that so bewitched me would be an enduring one.

II

Words are power.

This was what I learnt. Naturally timid and subject to ceaseless assault by my neighbours and classmates, I would grip the reins of my burgeoning vocabulary and feel a shot of self-esteem that made up for my crippling lack of courage. I was as yet unable to speak fluently, which won me unending mockery from my fellow students, who laughed not just at my poor Arabic but at my ethnic origins.

Generally speaking, in school as in wider society, there was a distinctly racist element in attitudes towards people from Eritrea and Ethiopia and their half-caste children, especially those born to non-Yemeni mothers. It was an attitude based first and foremost on skin colour. I was later to learn that this racism was actively encouraged by the regime of President Ali Abdullah Saleh, who came to power in 1978 when I was four years old; a regime based on a policy of divide and rule.

It left me with a deep-seated sense of humiliation and degradation that pushed me ever further into the embrace of cinema and language to soothe the psychological wounds I sustained in the real world. My progress through school was slow, marked by numerous failures. I repeated two years in primary and middle school. It was hard, but as a newcomer to the language, I had no choice.

Then I had a revelation. My talent for writing in Arabic would be my ticket out of the terminal state of weakness and vulnerability that left me exposed to daily humiliations. I decided to go to war against those who demeaned me and defeat them with their own language.

I would resort to writing.

III

In early 1990 I was just starting out as a journalist, working as a trainee at one of the newspapers that proliferated following the declaration of a free press. This declaration was itself a precursor to the process of national unification between tribal North Yemen, to which I belonged and which was ruled by Ali Abdullah Saleh, and an urbanized South Yemen under the control of the Yemeni Socialist Party.

I was still in high school at the time and this job was an opportunity to learn how to write professionally. The paper where I worked was loyal to the Socialist Party. There, I found, I was able to give voice to my hopes that tallied both with the slogans of the political Left and the aspirations of a whole generation of Yemenis who longed for freedom, civil rights and a life of dignity. I had sent a sample of my writing to the editors and they had accepted it for publication. We maintained contact and soon they had taken me on as a trainee journalist.

By mid-1990 Yemen was unified, Saleh was president of the new republic and the former president of South Yemen, Ali Salem al-Beid, had agreed to be his deputy. For the majority of Yemenis this unity had long been a distant dream, but it had only been in existence for a few weeks when President Saleh's true intentions began to emerge. Saleh wanted to control the South and appropriate its resources and he calmly set out to achieve his goal, working simultaneously on a number of different fronts.

Everything the President did suggested that he had no intention of allowing two different power bases to coexist at the summit of the new republic. Seeking to unseat his rivals and remain as sole leader of the country he proceeded to do all in his power to draw Yemen into civil war.

He sidelined the political leadership of the South, denied Southerners their rights and appropriated their property and land, redistributing it to tribal leaders and regime figures from the North. Inhabitants of the South wanted revenge, sensing that unification had benefitted the North at their expense, not to mention the fact that the President abolished all the manifestations of civil society that had made the South unique. Tribal values were promoted and weapons could be carried in the street, which jarred with a society that had always been peaceful, confident in the law's ability to defend their rights, without need for the gun-toting culture of the North, where the law's absence required citizens to take matters into their own hands.

Saleh also worked to promote sectarian divisions, amplifying them by throwing money at the warring parties. He would fund one side and then the other then sit back to watch a vicious war break out between them. This is how he was able to remain in power so long.

The socialist newspaper came into being in the midst of these changes. I was the youngest writer there, but the senior journalists took me under their wing. Most of them were highly educated Marxists, humble and unselfish. I learnt much from them. They pointed me towards books I should read, though they were never heavy-handed in their suggestions, and they introduced me to a large circle of writers and authors, whose friendship I treasure to this day and who taught me how to live a life that was different from the norm. They helped me and I still owe them a great debt.

Alongside the intellectual stimulus of my work at the paper I received the financial support of my monthly salary. It wasn't much, true, but it was enough to finish my studies and enough to make me feel that life was still possible, that I could pursue my dreams all the way.

But it became apparent that Saleh was not going to leave me to my own devices. He declared war in mid-1994, occupying the South and defeating the Socialist Party. Everything was finished, or so I believed. Its property stolen by the regime, the paper shut down, and once more I found myself broken, defeated and without hope. Worse, I was a known employee of the Socialist Party through my work at the paper. In the region where I lived agents for the regime had been hunting down and detaining anyone who had belonged to the Socialist Party or getting them fired from their jobs. Although I had not been a party member myself, just worked at a party newspaper, the regime made no distinction. My mother intervened, however, and hid me. She wouldn't let me out of the house.

My mother always protects me.

IV

I left high school about a year before civil war broke out and two months after it was over I was due to go to university.

I was broken and utterly alone. I had virtually no friends: everybody I knew had been scattered by the war and some had been killed, and as a 'socialist' I was shunned. People were afraid to be associated with me. The President's victorious party had little sympathy for 'fifth columnists' who maintained relationships with an 'enemy' from the Yemeni Socialist Party.

But despite my isolation I still had to enroll at university, if only for my mother's sake, who needed to see me get my degree so she could feel she hadn't given up her own life for nothing.

It was no easy task to move beyond the pain, oppression and humiliation with which racism had blighted my life. Some part of it would always stay with me, an obstacle to my smooth progress through life. Even now I can hear them whispering to each other, making fun of my strange accent and dark skin; I can feel the blows inflicted on my skinny body by those horrible boys as I did nothing but cry. I have words: my gift from the heavens, the lifebelt that will carry me safe to the other shore. Language will carry me forward, profound and powerful, I would whisper to myself incessantly so I wouldn't forget and lose heart. The memory of those black days keeps coming back to me, like the flickering reel of a horror film that never seems to end. Despite everything, I made it through high school; I stumbled many times, but I made it through and then I entered life: I entered university.

It was a new world, that would force me to confront an openly racist environment, where my dark skin was held in contempt. It was a confrontation that could not be avoided if I was to press forward and take the degree that would equip me to shoulder the burdens of the years ahead and fulfill the dreams of my Eritrean mother, who had sacrificed her life for our sake and left her homeland to accompany us to Yemen.

V

I entered university defeated, worn out and blinded. I simply could not see. I was like a man who has spent 20 years living in the dark confines of a prison and now must leave and learn to live all over again. It was in this state that I began at the Faculty of Languages, studying French. I have no idea why I chose French; all I remember is the moment the official handed me a form on which I had to put my three choices in order. Since high school I had always wanted to study philosophy, so why I put French as my first choice and philosophy as my second, I have no idea. I don't recall what my third choice was. With one stroke of the pen I consigned my dream of philosophy to the wastepaper basket where it joined all those other dreams, screwed up and discarded by the war. Just one more lost opportunity. Nothing mattered any more.

When the results of the selection appeared a few days later and I saw that I'd been accepted by the French department, I couldn't have cared less.

The French department had an atmosphere quite distinct to the rest of the university. Even the students seemed to have fallen from an alien, bourgeois planet. The way they dressed and acted made it clear that they came from rich backgrounds, and I stood out like a sore thumb. Of course this placed an additional burden on my shoulders and even my mother couldn't help me with this one. She had promised to take care of my basic expenses and there was no way I could ask her to spend money on my personal appearance. I had to find some regular, part-time work, in the evening if possible, and after some considerable effort I got a job at a restaurant located in an area far from where I lived. I had to do this because if my friends found out they would certainly tell my mother. This would cause her unnecessary pain, and she would forbid me from doing it. Luckily, no one ever found out and I worked there for two years and made good money.

While all this was going on I managed to pass my first year exams, though not without difficulty. I was the student with the lowest pass mark, understandably, since all the others had studied French at school. But I passed and was through to the second year. I will never forget the wonderful way I was treated by the staff of the department, most of whom were French or from other Arab countries. They were always smiling at me, as though they possessed some special ability to perceive the pain that lurked within me.

The racism continued at university, with some of the Yemeni students seemingly provoked by my easy manner, especially with the female students. I was constantly subjected to these irritations but I did not rise to them, preoccupied as I was with my studies.

I passed my second year. I found the work very difficult but I passed. It was at this point that I gave up my job at the restaurant for a chance to work at a major government newspaper, selecting and translating texts from French literary magazines for a weekly cultural supplement, and for a decent salary as well. I will never forget my time there, nor the people I worked with, especially the paper's owner, without whose support and understanding I would never have completed my degree. My colleagues were like a second family and we remain in touch to this day.

VI

As I made my way through university I never stopped thinking about the damage President Saleh had inflicted on my life. Slowly but surely the seed of hatred he had planted inside me grew.

It created in me something like a reverse racism against everyone whose skin was different to mine or who belonged to the ruling party; against Saleh and his family who had turned Yemen into a jungle inferno, fertile ground for the racism that robbed me of my rights just because my mother wasn't Yemeni. I was like a zombie, thinking only of revenge.

Whenever I saw him on television, speaking at some official celebration or government meeting, a fire would catch in my mind. His poor Arabic made me scream, littered with contradictions that stemmed from his appalling grammar and often unintelligible as a result.

As I listened to him speak I would ask myself in amazement how an idiot like this could end up ruling a country as large as Yemen. Wasn't there anyone better? It was clear that Saleh himself was well aware of his limitations and knew he had come to power almost by chance. Everything he did, all his policies, sprang from a desire to wreak personal vengeance, a profound psychological insecurity that led him to perform irrational acts as an expression of enmity and contempt towards Yemen and Yemenis. He nurtured corruption, despised education and deliberately laid waste to all aspects of civilized life, shutting down cinemas, theatres, bars and cultural clubs. Indeed, the vast majority of his policies were little more than an expression of his desire to destroy and corrupt everything in the country, to leave it in ruins. He appointed corrupt imbeciles to important positions in the universities with the sole aim of obliterating education and he got his wish. Did this stem from some ungovernable complex of his own? Was it because he had been unable to complete his own education, because he came from a tribal background of a particularly low social standing? His background, in fact, was the lowest of the low, a group that performed demeaning services for other tribesmen and functioned as their dogsbodies and servants. Yet others have come from similar backgrounds and managed to elevate themselves socially, without the insecurities that pushed Saleh to seek vengeance on society.

I could not get past it. I admit it: my hatred grew inside me. During my three years at university I was gripped by an overwhelming desire for revenge. I was yet to reconcile myself with the unfairness of life and I began to despise everything around me. I became a hateful person. I was that person and I must admit it. I will never be ashamed to tell the story of my life.

So I graduated and did so with distinction. I hadn't failed a single test in my last two years. My success had cost me much pain and effort but it gave me the chance to apply for the position of assistant lecturer at the university. They gave it to a colleague who had got better marks, but at the time I didn't care. I just wanted to see the joy on my mother's face, now that the success she had waited for for so long had become reality.

I was triumphant, but my old fears remained. I was still a coward. The dust of the past lay in a thick layer over my eyes and prevented me seeing clearly.

In my last year I had taken part in an annual short story competition for students at the university. I had been honing my writing skills for the previous two years and my grasp of

Arabic was now very good, but it was still a pleasant surprise when I was declared the winner. My first prize meant that after I graduated I was nominated to represent Yemen at a cultural competition for Arab youth held by the Arab League in the Egyptian city of Alexandria, where I shared second place with a young Egyptian woman. It was the first time I felt that I was a Yemeni citizen and that I represented Yemeni youth, particularly when the papers back home carried the news of my success. When I went back home, I thought, doors will start opening for me. Little did I know that my return would bring fresh torments.

I don't deny that at the same time I felt as though I had gained a first victory over Saleh. It was enough that I had got my wish and met the famous authors I had always longed to meet. And yet …

When I returned from Alexandria I found myself unable to get a job with my degree. I tried to get work as a guide for French tourists, but I was also unsuccessful. Life went on as usual. Saleh was increasing his powers and extending his control of the country and its people.

The days dragged by, as I woke each morning to find myself with no fixed employment, while others went busily about their working day. I went back to work at the cultural supplement; it was the only way I could make enough money to let me get on with my life. Through my work translating French literary texts I was offered the chance to travel to France, funded by the French embassy. It would be a three month residency, time enough to acquaint myself with a whole new world and improve my language skills.

It was during my stay in France that I was offered the opportunity to move to Holland and apply for refugee status. Many Yemenis had done just this, but not only did I lack the courage to take this step, the thought of abandoning my mother frightened me, and when the three months was up I returned home.

VII

Once back, I returned to my life of unemployment and poverty: no income and no job, save my part-time work for the newspaper. While my name was now well known my financial situation was at rock bottom.

I was doing well as a journalist, too, but I was poor, I was no longer that young and I had a degree: things couldn't go on this way. Life had to give me a break.

For five long years after graduating I lived this agony every day: invisible, with only writing and translation to sustain me. I wrote about culture and film, something I sorely missed now that Saleh had closed all the cinemas in Sanaa. I also started writing again for the newspaper of the Socialist Party, but for free this time: the party was in dire straits and couldn't afford to pay its journalists.

One evening I happened to meet the cultural attaché of the French embassy at the house of a friend who worked for the Yemeni foreign ministry. We talked for a long time and he told me that they were working to set up a French language department at a university in a city close to Sanaa. He asked if I was qualified to work as a university lecturer and offered me a job. I replied that I was technically qualified, but that people such as myself were effectively barred from university positions. I told him my story from start to finish. I had no idea at the time, but that evening was to open the door to new hope, and another door that led to hell.

The university, as expected, wanted to refuse my application, but the embassy intervened very forcefully, making their support of the study programme conditional on my being accepted. And so it came to pass: I was a university lecturer at long last.

Early each morning I made the journey from Sanaa to the university, returning at midday to the newspaper where I worked. For a time, my life was settled and I felt that at last I had got my foot on the first rung of the ladder. Then something happened to make me slip off once again.

A conference was held in Sanaa to promote inter-cultural dialogue. It was attended by Günter Grass, Mahmoud Darwish, Adonis, a large contingent of Arab and German writers and the Yemeni intellectual Jarallah Omar, a leading figure in the Yemeni Socialist Party, who I had known for a while before the civil war. About two weeks after the conference Jarallah Omar was murdered, killed by an extremist from one of Yemen's religious parties. Investigations revealed that the killer was a member of an extremist gang that had drawn up a hit list of 36 individuals – authors, intellectuals, journalists and academics – adjudged to be enemies of Islam.

My name was among them.

My days were transformed, fragmented into moments of sheer terror. I walked the streets expecting my killer to appear on every corner, waiting for the bullet to fly from the revolver concealed in the pocket of each and every passer-by.

It was a truly terrifying time.

Once again I was driven to shield myself with words, confronting the killers and showing them that I was not scared, despite the fear that lurked inside me, that had never left me. Words were my weapons.

I began to write about politics. I wrote about the political corruption that had allowed these fundamentalists to achieve prominence and kill people. Subsequently, newspaper reports would show that the killer was in fact backed by the regime.

It was during this period that a group of young journalists came to the fore, who would champion honest writing and freedoms in the country. One of these individuals was a young woman called Tawakkol Karman, who would win the Nobel Peace Prize in 2011. The new atmosphere they created emboldened me, despite the fears and misgivings that had beset me since childhood.

We wrote about everything, about the corruption of the President and his family, their theft of public funds and the networks of mutual interest they had extended over the country until they had come to own practically everything. We wrote about Saleh's eldest son, Ahmed Ali, and the gang he led, whose corrupting influence had penetrated into every aspect of public life. Thanks to these articles, we managed to raise people's awareness, if only a little, and the population began to feel that the President and his family were no longer sacred figures who could never be criticized.

As was to be expected, this meant that a number of us were subjected to physical assault, kidnappings, torture, trials and imprisonment. There was an attempt to assassinate me by running me down with a truck. I was hit, but by some miracle survived with only cuts and bruises. As a result I was forced to stop writing for a while. Strange to say, I was thinking about my mother at the moment the truck ran me over. She had been abroad for two months, visiting her family in Eritrea.

Just the thought of her was enough to keep me safe.

VIII

As the journalism became more incisive the public's consciousness slowly expanded, until Saleh completely changed the nature of the game and started preparing the way for his son Ahmed to succeed him as president once he had returned from his military training overseas. First, he was elected to parliament and then he was appointed Commander of the Republican Guard, the largest and most important military force in the country. He now had significant powers, enough to buy the loyalty he needed. Portraits of Ahmed began to appear alongside those of his father in the streets: a message to citizens that here was their next president.

Ahmed Ali Abdullah Saleh held the keys to the kingdom. Being close to Ahmed was a guarantee of an important position in government and the regime's senior players started to curry favour with him, knowing that he had the power to change their lives.

It was increasingly apparent that Yemen was heading towards a succession of power, transforming from a republic into a monarchy with a meaningless republican veneer and Ahmed as its 'crown prince'. It was the same scenario that was playing out in Syria with Bashar al-Assad, with Saif al-Islam al-Gaddafi in Libya and Gamal Mubarak in Egypt. If they could do it, why shouldn't Saleh's kid be king?

My bile would rise whenever I considered that my future happiness was in the hands of an individual scarcely older than myself, whose only qualification was being born the son of a president. I watched as my colleagues at university ingratiated themselves with the new status quo by talking about Ahmed in glowing terms, and I realized I was right. Our future was in his hands. It was as though they knew their words would reach the ledgers of the security services and be entered as credit against their names.

I had nothing but contempt for my fellow professors who stooped to such shameful tactics just to get promoted at the university or advance through the ranks of the ruling party. I had thought that the 'Dr' before their names was a guarantee that they would conduct themselves with dignity and honour, if nothing else, out of respect for the generous salary they received at the end of every month.

This contempt, that started out as sarcastic jibes to my colleagues, gradually crept into my writing. I wrote a number of articles about 'Ahmed Ali', the most prominent of which had this shortened form of his name as its title, though the edition of the weekly supplement that contained it was not allowed to be printed. The piece contained harsh, though civilly-worded criticism of the new realities. An old friend who worked for one of the State's security agencies told me the article had provoked a considerable reaction in the presidential office, and they were seriously displeased with me, but I didn't care. I considered what I had written to be the truth and it contained nothing that should be punishable by law. I also considered such forceful writing to be a kind of protection in itself, a veil over my cowardice and fear. If I wrote like that they would think I was brave and wouldn't notice the terror that crawled beneath my skin.

Then my friend told me something else. They had put me on the blacklist and they would have their revenge. It was only later that the truth of this became apparent and I saw how long their memories were.

IX

An end, or at least a response, to the corruption and injustice practised by Saleh and his family was an inevitability. He regarded Yemen and the Yemeni people as his personal fiefdom and now he wanted to pass them on to his son.

It was scarcely credible, indeed, it made no sense at all, that the standard of living in the country could continue to fall while the people looked on silently. Complaints were growing and everyone was muttering about their discontent and their fears for the future. Certainly Ahmed did not inspire hope: he did not care and no one could get close to him. He had come to think of himself as a god, and who can stand before a god?

But the cup was running over and a single drop would send an uncontainable flood of rage spilling out. And this is what happened.

The Arab Spring arrived. Tunisia's president was toppled and fled and the next morning the students of Sanaa University took to the streets in celebration. There weren't many of them, but the slogans they chanted still had the power to shock, calling for equality, freedom, social justice, and above all, the fall of the regime. Just like that: without any of the warning signs and build-up we witnessed in Tunisia and Egypt, where calls for the regime to go only started after protestors had been fired on and killed. In this respect, the students of Sanaa were unique, marching straight out onto the street from their classrooms and chanting, 'The people demand the fall of the President and the regime.'

Maybe they knew it was pointless asking Saleh for political and economic reforms. He had become addicted to corruption and it was too late for him to break the habit.

The day the students filled University Square I was profoundly happy, full of a joy I had not felt for many long years. At the same time I feared for my heart, that it would be swayed by this joy, caught up in a feeling that was destined not to last and which would fizzle and die like all those moments of hope. My soul was not strong enough to bear another setback and defeat. I was still getting over another piece of traumatic news that had painted my eyes black and left me blind: they had carried out their threat and punished me, removing me from my position at the university without giving any reasons, in clear contravention of the law. But what was law? The only law in this bandit country was the law of President Saleh.

So I was blind, broken and defeated, utterly alone and forsaken. No one stood by me or defended me and there I was, unemployed again. When the Arab Spring came to Yemen I couldn't help but be drawn to it, setting out to take part despite my ever-present fears and my concern that the students would soon get bored and go home. But far from it. Their number grew and the protests swelled, spreading to cities outside Sanaa. The 'Square of Change' was now home to thousands of young people, joined by large numbers of young tribesmen who travelled to Sanaa to take part in the revolution.

Hope started to grow inside me, but there was pain, too. The hardest thing the revolution had to face in the beginning was the mockery directed at it by Arab writers and intellectuals, who found it hilarious that such a thing should be attempted in Yemen, and regarded our young people as poorly equipped for a revolution when compared with their contemporaries in Tunisia and Egypt.

'They're armed tribesmen,' they would say: 'They only understand guns and bullets and fire! How can they be expected to see the point of peaceful protests or have a peaceful revolution? These people live in the Stone Age. What do they know of the internet or Facebook?'

They were merciless, but quickly changed their tune when they saw these young people in Freedom Squares the length and breadth of Yemen, making the impossible real and stunning the world: 'The youth of Yemen have done it: created an astonishing example of civil activism. No one dreamt it was possible.'

So declared Qatar's *Al Jazeera*, adding: 'Most of us did not hold out much hope that young people accustomed to using guns and with ready access to them, would not fire a single shot to defend themselves from attack by the security forces of President Saleh's regime.'

Though many of us were killed and Saleh used every brutal tactic in the book to break the sit-in and defeat the revolution, we did not fire a single bullet in response. I lost many friends, people I had known from school and university. In just one incident alone snipers killed 56 young men, the gunmen positioned on high buildings overlooking the Square of Change firing into the massed protestors. *Al Jazeera* carried footage of the massacre to the world.

From afar, I watched my colleagues fall one after the other. I lacked the courage to take part and protect them. I'm just a writer, I told myself, my job is to write. That is how I always justify my cowardice to myself: I'm no hero and I never will be.

X

The revolution gathered pace. Nine months of struggle and astonishing acts of heroism while Saleh continued to murder and burn and I did nothing but write. The longer Saleh persisted with this killing the harder it was for the world to stand by and watch. The Security Council intervened and issued warnings to the President, but it was not enough to stem the flow of blood. It became obvious that certain Western and Arab states were reluctant to remove this man and plunge Yemen into chaos or hand it over to al-Qaeda, a scenario that Saleh himself used to hold the world to ransom.

'It's me or al-Qaeda,' he'd tell them: 'If I go then who will stop them?'

And they listened, even though they knew that he was sheltering and protecting the members of this terrorist gang and using them to scare the West.

Then there was Yemen's neighbour, Saudi Arabia. The kingdom's princes were troubled by the thought of a revolution that might threaten their interests in the country and the emergence of a new generation of leaders who would end their comfortable relationship with Saleh and their control of Yemeni politics. The Saudis have fought every revolution in the Arab world, so of course they would take on a revolution in Yemen that had the potential to spread to their soil.

However, as Saleh continued to kill, these countries had no choice but to issue a forceful declaration to show that they were not in favour of Saleh's relentless, murderous campaign to ignite a civil war in Yemen. They proposed an initiative that apparently offered a solution to the situation, though in reality it was just a lifebelt for Saleh. The Saudi proposal was to remove Saleh from power, without affecting powers of the regime, his son Ahmed, his relatives or the army. It was designed to give him immunity, to protect him from being tried under international law for the murder of young protestors.

Saleh did indeed step down, but the regime and his appointed successor Ahmed remained in place. The revolutionaries refused to accept this, demanding the removal of the entire regime and for Saleh to be tried for crimes against humanity in the International Criminal Court. It was inconceivable that the man who had killed all those young people could be allowed to escape punishment. It was simply unjust.

So the young revolutionaries fight on, until all their demands are met and they are free to build their State: a state founded on social justice and equality between all citizens where Saleh's reign is just a page in the history books.

XI

As for me, well I'm still going, writing about the revolution and the amazing young people who have astonished the world with their peaceful struggle. I can say, with just a hint of pride, that I have played my part from afar in the construction of this noble, humanist endeavour.

I'm still unemployed, still trying to get my life back on track. I live with my mother. She recently found out that I'd been fired from the university, but she was happy anyway, happy that I'm still alive.

Each morning I get up to write some more. The act of writing, words themselves, are the way I stop myself drowning in the fear that follows me every second of every day: a crushing fear of the world and everyone in it, a savage illness that holds me in its jaws and never lets me go. The fear from which I shall never be free.

Sanaa
December 2011

6

COMING DOWN FROM THE TOWER (BAHRAIN)

By Ali Aldairy
Translated from the Arabic by Robin Moger

Bahrain is a small island some 750 square kilometres in size, ruled by the tribe of al-Khalifa. In 1783 the al-Khalifa 'liberated' Bahrain (or invaded: the difference in terminology remains a political issue to this day), treating it as spoils of war, which they had the right to do with as they wished.

In 1923 the British colonial power imposed political reforms and the mechanisms of State began to take shape.* Extremist factions within al-Khalifa and the allied tribes with whom they had conquered Bahrain rejected these reforms, which sought to establish a degree of parity between the tribes and the indigenous Shia inhabitants. The transformation into a modern state never happened and the tribal system of governance remained an influential part of the nation's system of government.

---

* Bahrain was from the early nineteenth century until 1971 a protectorate of the British Empire; in 1783 it was 'liberated' from its status as a dependency of the Persian Empire.

In 1971 Bahrain declared independence and in 1973, youthful opposition forces pushed through the drafting of a written constitution and the formation of a democratic parliament. The experiment was aborted by the authorities: in 1975 the parliament was dissolved, the 1973 constitution was abrogated and the country was placed under emergency law; patriotic politicians and activists were jailed.

In 2001 the National Action Charter was brought out and a year later, without any public consultation, the King issued a new constitution and foisted a parliament with curtailed powers on the country. The government was left unchanged. The post of prime minister has been held by Khalifa Bin Salman al-Khalifa from the date of Bahrain's independence in 1971 until the present day.

With the uprising of February 14, 2011, the country entered another crisis. One of the protestors' main demands was the formation of a government elected by the people. This demand constituted a serious threat to the regimes of all the conservative Gulf states, none of whom had ever experienced anything resembling an elected government. Under the banner of the Peninsula Shield forces they intervened to discipline this revolutionary democratic movement and on 16 March they 'purged' Pearl Square, the site of the protestors' sit-in.

The February 14 Revolution and me

In this account, which is as much personal record as it is objective history, I would like to talk about the events shaping my sense of self through the events shaping my country; the narrative of self and state become one.

At its core the Bahrain revolution is about two things: state and sect. How does a sect make the transition to a state? How does the state become a system of governance capable of incorporating a number of sectarian groups with different (if not openly contradictory) cultures, interests and historical narratives? This is the challenge that Bahrain faced on 14 February, and now that day is part of the country's journey from sect to state, from tribe to country.

I want to tell the story of the formation of the February 14 movement as an attempt to break free from sectarianism and tribalism and operate in the framework of a modern state, and of the challenges this movement faced.

So as not to betray

An account of my own experience with this movement should begin with a look at my cultural role. A few days prior to February 14 I tweeted: 'I am a Bahraini writer and intellectual. What does that mean now? Can someone help me?'

'It means you should do your job: i.e. criticism,' came one response.

'Criticize what?' I asked.

'Criticize erroneous thinking, of course. In other words, the intellectual's task is to make logical, reasoned thought possible within society.'

'My friend,' I wrote, 'I'm looking for an answer that will save me from the list of shame.'

At that moment, with a revolutionary movement about to break out, I was thinking how I might avoid becoming a traitor to its cause. French philosopher Julien Benda's *La Trahison des Clercs* came to mind: when the intellectual sheds his morals and principles, he betrays. When it came to this revolution that was about to erupt in Bahrain, I asked myself, would I betray, or would I be a true intellectual, carrying out his duty as a moralist and freedom fighter. I use the term freedom fighter not in its purely political sense, but culturally, to mean that the intellectual should always be fighting for freedom, for humanity; to liberate the mind and enable peaceful coexistence.

I was worried, and the subsequent unfolding of events justified my concern. Many intellectuals would betray their duty to society and these betrayals eventually led me to resign from the Family of Authors and Writers (Bahraini writers' union) in a letter that made repeated reference to this bad faith. I wrote: 'Culture does not automatically give rise to good; the immorality of cultural circles no longer surprises us.' (Tzvetan Todorov)

'I resign, because nothing surprises me any more.'

And it was this worry of mine that led me to try and get a better sense of what might take place on 14 February and later to participate in events. There was a significance to what happened from the very beginning, not because the movement itself was that powerful but because the repression it faced from the first day was so brutal. The protests stirred the street but it was blood that set it alight.

Blood

From 28 January 2011 (a turning point in the Egyptian uprising) onwards, Bahraini discussion groups began addressing the idea of a revolution in light of what had taken place in Tunisia and Egypt. The protests that took to the streets in 25 provinces marched beneath the Bahraini national flag and chanted for political reform, the release of prisoners and other demands related to the standard of living. Their slogan mimicked the Egyptians' before them, only one word was different: 'The people demand the *reform* of the regime'.

From the moment they began to march, on the evening of 14 February, they were subjected to violent repression by the security forces. Soon, shockingly soon, police shotguns caused the death of the first martyr: 21-year-old Ali Mushaima. The protest instantly transformed into a solid mass of rage.

We had yet to recover from the shock when, on the morning of 15 February the security forces killed their second victim,

Fadil al-Matrouk, 32, as he left home to join the funeral procession of the first, and wounded tens more, some severely, with baton strikes and shotgun fire.

The anger intensified. Crowds gathered outside Manama's Salmaniya Hospital near to where al-Matrouk was killed. The chants were harsher now: 'The people demand the fall of the regime!'

The situation evolved as rapidly as the slogan had. The afternoon of the same day, the King appeared on television to voice his sorrow at what had happened:

> Sadly, two of our dear sons met their end, for which we extend our sincerest condolences to their families and may the Sublime and Omnipotent grant them patience, peace of mind and comfort in their grief. We hereby announce that the Deputy Prime Minister, His Excellency Jawad Bin Salim al-Arid, has been tasked by us with forming a dedicated committee to look into the causes of these regrettable incidents.

The committee, created that day by royal decree, seemed to have fulfilled its mandate in the very act of being announced to the public. From that day, neither hide nor hair has been seen of it, less still a result. It is just the regime playing its ridiculous game of make-believe accountability.

That evening Pearl Square thronged with angry crowds, come to bear their rage aloft, to shout it out in this public space. Tens of thousands flocked to the square and this time the security forces did not stop them; the troops, who had withdrawn following the King's address, were nowhere to be seen. As night drew in tents were put up and preparations made for a sit-in that would last, they declared, until their demands were met.

Liberating the square

Believe me, when I left home that afternoon I had no intention of going to Pearl Square. I was going to the Jadhafas cemetery where Ali Mushaima was buried and where a reporter I know, Abdel Wahhab al-Arid, was waiting for me.

When I got there I found a crowd heading towards the square, and we allowed ourselves to be swept up, following their footsteps as they blazed a new path to freedom. Walking along at 2:30 on that winter afternoon was delightful. We took souvenir snaps to show to those who hadn't made it to the square then we were stopped by a group of women scattering a kind of basil scent called *mashmum* on the marcher's feet. It was a moment both intimate and meaningful.

Arriving at the square at precisely 2:50 p.m. on 15 February came as a great surprise to all. No one had expected to make it. I took a photo on my iPhone and sent it to my contacts using WhatsApp. 'We're now in the heart of Pearl Square waiting for the response of the regime's forces,' I wrote. This was the first message I sent to my friends on Twitter and WhatsApp, hoping to convey the symbolism of our attempt to liberate a public, participatory space where people had come to build the state and the system of governance they wanted.

As I typed out my message, onions rolled back and forth. Bahrainis have used onions against tear gas since protests first flared up in the 1980s, as confrontations with the security forces are much older than the current uprising. The protestors were practising their kicking skills, with these onions. It wasn't the heads of the security troops they were thinking of, but tear gas canisters. A few moments later I heard chanting coming from the edge of the square. Ibrahim Sharif, general secretary of the Waad Party, was being carried on the shoulders of protestors, waving a Bahraini flag with one hand and with the other gesturing at the crowds and proclaiming his solidarity with their cause.

The sun shone down and the white of Pearl Monument gleamed brightly. Some protestors took a nap on the grass, tired after a long and exhausting morning; some quick shut-eye after the shock of their success.

The meaning of the square gradually took shape in my mind. Prior to today, Pearl Square had been no more than a busy roundabout constantly choked with circling cars, but now it had become a place of defiance. We had come here to challenge the regime's own gridlock, the congestion caused by corruption, preferential treatment, violence, tyranny, the absence of citizens' rights and the prevalence of artificially propagated loyalist parties. Tens of thousands of disgusted citizens had come to assemble and chant and give voice to their anger.

A test of tolerance

As the shadows lengthened, Pearl Square became a public square, no longer the patch of ground around which cars coursed in search of an exit. It was a place where people came to condemn the agencies of State that had worn them out, making them circle endlessly about a wasteland devoid of meaning.

The square became a stage. First to speak was the lawyer Hassan Rida, who said the people were asking for a constitution based on public consultation and a democratic government controlled by the people in accordance with a constitution that protected the diverse and differing communities that made up the population.

My friend, the British academic and intellectual Adrian Alan Brockett had insisted on attending. Parking his car at the Regency Hotel he walked the 800 metres to the roundabout, finally arriving at exactly 11 o'clock. I was waiting for him with a group of friends and when he saw me he exclaimed in astonishment: 'This is unbelievable! All these crowds of protestors in a public square; people from all walks of life with their slogans, signs and chants!'

I explained that of all the Gulf states only in Bahrain would this be possible, and it was this that gave the events in Pearl Square their impact: it was a direct assault on the status quo in the Gulf, a system based on unswerving loyalty and obedience to the authorities in return for a guaranteed income.

By the following day, 16 February, the square surged with humanity and diversity. The demonstrators, Sunni and Shia together, performed the afternoon prayers together then painted the Pearl Monument, covering the raging graffiti they had scrawled the day before. They restored its pristine whiteness and if anything their sheer enthusiasm made it shine brighter than before.

The square was now a true experiment, a test of coexistence between the different factions who had turned up. This was the greatest challenge of all, the real *jihad*: how to make the square a truly common ground, a public space where the patriotism that bound us could flourish and the differences fade away.

At that time, reality still fell short of our expectations but the dream was clearly taking shape: the square was an experiment and the experiment a test that would teach us how we might live side by side despite our disagreements.

An anthem incomplete

I soon found myself part of the square and found, too, that as much as it was an experiment for coexistence, it confronted me with another kind of test: an opportunity for myself as an intellectual to apply my theoretical understanding of concepts like freedom, humanity, public space, common ground, the state, plurality and democracy. I had to approach the reality on the ground through the theories peddled by the books of major thinkers and apply them to lived experience. I was eager to use every invention of modern communication technology to convey the full experience of these moments; to become an observer, broadcasting these events with a critical, observant eye.

I sent quotes from speeches over Twitter occasionally accompanied by my critique of what was being said. I made a record of anything I heard or saw that stood at odds with the idea of a civil state.

The night of 16 February I settled down on the grass, put my computer on my lap and wrote down all these observations of mine and an account of my experiences and when I got home just before one in the morning I sent the file to friends and to a number of email lists that included the country's political, media and intellectual elite. At that time I had no idea that the first news of the atrocity would reach me in just a few hours.

I dozed off and was woken at four in the morning to hear what had happened: riot troops supported by the army had attacked the roundabout at 2:30 a.m. leaving dead and wounded in their wake. How was I meant to absorb the shock? We had just been there ourselves, hymning freedom, celebrating plurality and diversity. They had all been fast asleep, peaceful as a dream. How dare they?

Two dead, it was said, and hundreds wounded; the medical tent had not been spared, nor the doctors themselves. Dr Sadiq al-Akri was assaulted and beaten, afforded no protection by his white uniform and cries that he was a doctor. He collapsed and was taken to the emergency ward.

We swapped information.

The injured had taken refuge in the Salmaniya Hospital compound on the grounds that medical facilities would be inviolate and safe.

The staff were in shock.

No one knew the number of wounded or the nature of their injuries.

New cases started arriving at the hospital in private vehicles; the ambulances that had left to transport the wounded had vanished.

Crowds and mob anger.

The protestors attempted to return to the roundabout.

The security forces met them with tear gas, firing baton rounds and rock salt from point-blank range.

The head of a third martyr received a direct hit and was blown apart, an incident witnessed by the journalist Naziha Saeed and which later appeared in the media.

Security troops advanced towards the hospital compound from the square, preventing ambulances from reaching the roundabout and assaulting their crews.

The intellectual's test

I couldn't stay home any more. Leaving the house I headed for Salmaniya Hospital and arrived in time to see the doctors set out, marching to protest against the actions of health minister Faisal al-Hamar and his team in preventing ambulances from reaching the roundabout and rescuing the wounded. The place was throbbing with rage, chaotic and explosive and traumatized by an attack that had come just two days after the King's apology. There I stood, observing the injured bodies with my camera and all my senses. I saw tears, the impact this massacre had on people and on the chants they bellowed inside the hospital compound.

I was recording events on Twitter, trying to fulfill my duty as an intellectual; no longer sitting in my ivory tower, I was now in touch with the people. Twitter forced me go to the scene itself, to follow events with my own eyes, to record them and transmit them myself. I was face to face with the truth of what was happening.

Those intellectuals who were not face to face with this reality were very far away indeed. Geographically, Bahrain may be small but they were ever so distant because they drew their information from the State media, from the echoes of their ivory towers and their positions of influence in the State, however trifling the benefits they accrued.

What you are getting is not the truth; what you are getting is what they want you to hear. The poor and ignorant might be excused for falling for these games, these tricks and frauds, but the intellectual, who knows history and who knows about the brutality of regimes, has no excuse for accepting what he is told when only a footstep separates him from the scene itself. Some intellectuals set about lending the authorities' narrative a greater credibility by circulating slanders of a sectarian opposition.

For myself, therefore, Twitter was an incentive to visit the scene itself, instead of waiting for the news to reach me. I typed out messages choked with the shock and distress:

> Here at Salmaniya Hospital the medical teams are confused, the protestors are confused and the wounded are left waiting. Only the martyrs are confused no longer: they are perfectly at peace.
>
> Here in the emergency ward the scene is distressing, ridiculous, serious, farcical, desperate, hopeful ... Contradictions everywhere. We all wait for an ambulance to be allowed back from the square with a body, something like a body, no body at all: we just want it to come!
>
> Went into the morgue and photographed the bodies of the martyrs. The head of one has been pulverized. People are hysterical.

Off the page and into the field

Concerning the first assault on the roundabout, for Lebanese newspaper *an-Nahar*, I wrote:

> Thursday, February 17 was two days, not one: the early hours of the morning and the day that followed. Between these two the army's bullets sang. The army had succeeded in their mission impossible: they had fashioned for us a

second, unforgettable day out of a day that might have been forgotten. How magnificent you are, my army, discharger of feats unfeasible: you have made our day so very, very long. It is thanks to you that I – I, who was accustomed to the smell of books and paper, not the stench of the dead – walked into the morgue the following afternoon. It was the first time I had been into a morgue. I went because I needed to believe that you really had carried out your impossible task. I saw your glorious achievement inscribed on the bodies of the martyrs and I saw what your sightless war machine had not: I saw that you are not of my country; I saw that you are its shame.

So it was that I found myself outside the pages of my books inside the events themselves. I let myself go further in, to see more, to examine more. I chose not to be a paper intellectual, but a journalist in the field, confronting reality, testing it with every one of my senses. And I found myself at one with the people's demands for a constitutional monarchy, for an elected government, for a parliament in possession of a full complement of powers and for a constitution drawn up by the people.

A procession of blood and a procession of loyalty

Friday, 18 February was another long and terrible day.

At 1:30 in the afternoon the funeral of 22-year-old engineer Ali Ahmad al-Mumin took place. He had died after a shotgun round struck him in the hip, severing an artery. The efforts of Dr Sadiq Abdullah could not save him; 30 bags of blood failed to restore his pulse.

At around 5:30 that morning Ali had made his last entry on his Facebook page: My blood for my country.

Short hours later his words became reality, a truth that stunned his father, mother and six siblings when they received the news of his martyrdom.

Ali was in the final year of his engineering degree at the University of Bahrain. He had been with one of his brothers in Pearl Square, sleeping peacefully when the security forces attacked. Ali had made it out alive to make his final Facebook entry, then returned to the roundabout with his brother Hussein, where he was hit with baton rounds and internationally-outlawed shotgun shells. He died from his wounds and took his hopes and dreams with him.

I knew nothing about him. On Thursday evening I opened his Facebook page and my senses were penetrated by his glowing image. I sat frozen before the picture: from its depths something was calling me to write about him. I made an absurd attempt to add him as a friend, then even more absurdly I waited for him to accept my request, reloading the page and telling myself 'perhaps he might' or perhaps some supernatural force might do it on his behalf. I needed to speak to him: 'I want to write about that special light you have, the light that drew me to you. Tell me something of your life story, something I can open my book with.'

I hunted on the internet and found him on YouTube, alive and full of motion, introducing a voluntary workshop for the residents of Sitra (an island in the Central Governorate of Bahrain just east of Bahrain Island in the Persian Gulf), where he came from. Listening to the questions raised in the workshop I realized they were my questions as well: How are we different? How am I different from the people with whom I share my country, my village, my family and my faith? I got a sense of the broad and welcoming diversity he believed in.

On Friday afternoon I went to attend his funeral on the island of Sitra – the Sitra that was famed for its poverty, its history of political resistance, its courage and its kindness. I watched the awful procession bearing his funeral throne, the Bahrain flag wrapped about his tender young body and the young men clustered about his coffin waving more national flags in the air. They adored the flag these young men; they waved it aloft, walked behind it, liberated squares with it and then they died without it.

At the request of his grief-stricken mother the procession halted and the following words were sung:

> Mother, remember me by the young men marching [...] by the empty wedding throne. My wedding henna is the blood of the wounded. Who snuffed out the candle of my youth? My henna is my blood, the coffin a house of dust.

It was a painful moment, and I lived it like all the other moments, sent messages on Twitter like I always did. That inner voice was drawing me closer to these young men and I became increasingly certain that it was my special duty to write about Ali Ahmad al-Mumin.

While we were experiencing the pain of these moments, and on the same day that the funerals of four other victims of Thursday's violence were being held, our hearts still bruised and tender, another procession was setting out not far from where we stood, a triumphal march organized by regime loyalists at al-Fatih mosque. According to the narrative of the ruling family, they 'liberated' Bahrain (or conquered it, according to the narrative of Bahrain's Shia inhabitants) and so the mosque is thus a monument to the ruling family.

Calls by moderates to postpone the march out of respect for the feelings of the families of the dead and wounded went unheeded. They insisted on celebrating before the blood had dried, before the victim's bodies had been committed to the earth. Many refused to participate. Attendance was low. As footage of the event revealed, the majority appeared to be foreign workers from south Asia, who were paid to celebrate. Nevertheless, the protestors feelings were still further inflamed that the regime could kill then celebrate its killing.

Live rounds

In the afternoon, my friend Abdel Wahhab and I left my house, in the Jabalat Habashi district, near Sanabis and not far from Pearl Square. It was the day of the memorial service (it's custom in many Muslim communities that services be held four days later) for the first martyr, Ali Mushaima, and we moved off in the direction of Jadhafas cemetery. On Twitter I wrote: 'Heading for the march from Jadhafas cemetery. The street's crowded and we haven't seen the cemetery yet.'

One of the marchers informed us that they were going to Pearl Square. We drove off to the square. Suddenly we heard the sound of gunshots and tear gas being fired. We went closer; the scene grew more confused; cars driving in the wrong direction. Abdel Wahhab got out of the car, approached a group of young men and started photographing the wounded as I drove on, unable to pull over in the midst of such chaos. I sent a series of tweets:

Heavy fire and ambulances carrying the injured, all heading for Salmaniya Hospital, which is already full to capacity.

Seriously injured man taken away on a pickup.

Car belonging to a member of parliament driving in front of me.

Journalist friend runs forward and says they're using live rounds.

Young man next to me weeping hysterically. Seems his friend has been badly hurt.

Stopped at an intersection in al-Naim. More than 8 ambulances have passed by.

It transpired that the mourners marched towards the round-about, which was surrounded by the army and security troops. The young men, their bodies wrapped in Bahrain flags, approached the armoured vehicles and the security forces and came to a halt some 100 metres away from them, shouting, 'In peace! In peace!' For a few minutes ... nothing ... then gunfire again filled the air. The scene was captured on film and viewed by the entire world: images of victims falling to the ground and the hail of live rounds, rubber bullets and tear gas that left the whole place and the people in it unable to breathe.

We made our way to the hospital. The streets were in wild disorder. The young men from the march were rushing back and forth to the hospital in their cars ferrying the wounded in the cars. An enraged crowd milled about outside the emergency ward and we joined a human chain clearing a path for the ambulances to arrive and carry the injured inside.

People were shouting hysterically. Their numbers swelled and so did the volume of their angry screams and wails, their chants demanding the fall of the regime. I tweeted:

> Outside the emergency ward at Salmaniya Hospital with press photographer Mazen Mahdi sobbing bitterly from everything his camera has witnessed. God be with you, Mazen. I wish I had the bravery of one of your photos.

As this was taking place, the Crown Prince stunned everyone with an unexpected television appearance in which he gave an apprehensive, impromptu address to the nation:

> I offer my condolences to all the people of Bahrain for the painful days through which we are living and I wish to send a message to everyone to remain calm. We need time to evaluate what has happened, to gather ourselves, to restore our humanity and civilized selves, to reclaim our future. Today we are at a crossroads. Young men are taking to the streets, believing that they have no future in this country; others are doing so out of love for their country and the desire to preserve its achievements. But this land belongs to all, not to one group or another. It does not belong to Sunni or Shia but to Bahrain and the people of Bahrain. At times such as these it is the duty of every true patriot to

say, 'Enough!' To regain what we have lost over the past few days will be no easy matter, but I have faith in the abilities of true-hearted men.

He delivered this speech, while in the streets outside the television studios it had been raining bullets.

In Salmaniya Hospital all doctors were summoned to the operating rooms. There were now 96 injured cases in the building, some with wounds from live rounds. According to medical sources at the scene, six were taken in for immediate surgical intervention. The most serious case was that of Abdel Rida Bouhamid (38 years old), who had been shot in the head and was now clinically dead. X-rays confirmed that a live round had penetrated his skull.

We stayed in the hospital until late into the night, where we got to know a group of British correspondents. We showed them some of the pictures and video clips we had taken. We viewed the X-rays of the martyr Abdel Rida. We all saw them with our own eyes. The doctor who talked us through them turned out to be an old acquaintance of mine from primary school. We came from the same village, had not seen each other since leaving school and now we met again over the fatal bullet lodged in Abdel Rida Bouhamid's head.

The list of shame

There was no space left for neutrality or professions of balance; no excuse for sitting behind one's desk and failing to go down to the street to see for oneself. Insensitivity, naivety, superficiality maybe, but never balance in that positive sense; the word can never be anything other than negative and terrifying. As Hannah Arendt writes in her book, *On Violence*:

'Detachment and equanimity' in view of 'unbearable tragedy' can indeed be terrifying, namely, when they are not the result of control but an evident manifestation of incomprehension. In order to respond reasonably one must first of all be 'moved'. (Arendt 1970, New York: Harvest Books, p.64)

Is the intellectual, the writer, the journalist, the opinion maker, not angered to witness the murder of those who took to the streets to peacefully demand their civil rights? This is a betrayal of humanity. Are they not roused to defend demands for political reform and a government elected by the people? This is a betrayal of the principles of freedom and democracy. Worse yet, these intellectuals rise up against the demonstrators themselves, pasting them with superficial labels like 'Shia' or 'religious', which strip them of their right to protest and reject. In doing so they betray their duty, which is to champion the rights of man regardless of his beliefs or faith.

On the morning of 19 February still dazed with terror at the things I had lived through over the past two days, I began searching through the national press for a voice that spoke up for humanity and the souls who had been lost. Turning to the dinosaurs who penned opinion pieces in the local papers I read the columns one by one. I turned to the eminent intellectuals and looked for a word repudiating murder and repression. Nothing.

Only *al-Wasat* bothered to convey what had happened and the whole paper was given over to exhaustive coverage of events, for which it later paid the price. On 2 and 3 April, the Information Ministry closed down the newspaper and its website, accusing it of 'misrepresentation and deliberate falsification of news'. (A 'trial' of the newspaper was televized on Bahraini TV and the ban lifted only after the resignation of its senior editorial staff.) And *al-Wasat* was working alone: the rest of my country's media made excuses for the massacre, instead soliciting the government for its explanation then adding its own fabrications. It recognized the legitimacy of the government's actions while denying the legitimacy of the dead and wounded's protest, accusing them of sectarianism and factionalism on the basis that the majority belonged to one religious group.

I watched as these established sages of the press lost what was left of their humanity, diligently patching up the ragged uniforms of loyalty and obedience that guaranteed them a comfortable way of life. These wordsmiths, some of whom had belonged to revolutionary movements in the 1970s, were so old now that they were no longer capable of understanding, let alone accepting, why young people would revolt and rise up to create a different tomorrow.

In my inbox I received a scanned document entitled 'The list of shame' containing the names of journalists who had described the protestors as traitors and Iranian agents, while praising the authorities' repressive response.

Following the entry of Saudi forces into the country and their 16 March assault on Pearl Square the true extent of this shame would become clearer and the need to generate a fraudulent justification for their support of the inhuman brutality even more pressing.

There would be a new wave of recruits to the list of shame, using all the techniques of dishonesty, selective reporting, special pleading and outright forgery to forge an even more powerful discourse of hatred.

This list, which those named persist in attributing to me despite my making it clear on Facebook that I received it via email, has been turned into a stick by the government and its supporters to beat me with, trumped up evidence used to condemn me as an intellectual. My crime? I declared my opposition to the scribblers who help the authorities murder, anathematize, torture, starve and divide the people, setting us against each other and inflaming civil strife.

The blossoming

On the afternoon of 18 February an incident of a completely different nature took place. Abdel Wahhab and I dropped in on the British correspondents we had met the night before and we took them from the Diplomat Hotel back to the hospital. It was just before two in the afternoon.

On the way we saw that groups of young men had taken to the streets to break the siege around Pearl Square. We followed them. One of our new friends, his journalistic instincts to the fore, said, 'This is where it'll happen.'

We expected to see the crowds edge closer to the barriers set up by the riot police some 500 metres from the side of the roundabout in the direction of Sanabis. There would be clashes with troops firing tear gas but avoiding the baton rounds and tactics that had caused so many injuries over the past few days.

The opposition activist Ibrahim Sharif, who is currently serving a five year prison sentence with 21 others for attempting to 'overthrow the regime', was the first politician to turn up and lend his support. Standing alongside the young men on the front line he turned to the security forces and asked their commander to permit a peaceful sit-in, informing him that no one had any intention of causing a disturbance. The security forces were responsive in what seemed to be the lead-up to a general withdrawal for which they were awaiting orders.

The young protestors, meanwhile, started to employ delightful tactics, almost flirting with the troops that faced them. Their bodies swathed in national flags, some sat on the ground holding their flags aloft while others approached the barrier carrying roses, which they passed to the troops through small holes in the fence, their stems proudly unbowed. Every outstretched rose sent an ever stronger message of peace, weakening the barricades before them, tempering the dread of the brutal machines of war and softening the severity in the soldiers' eyes.

We looked on with the frank astonishment and thrill of those witnessing a new beginning, a blossoming of roses to humble and defeat the burgeoning hostility. The wonderful weather only heightened the splendour of the scene.

Via Twitter I reported on it all and received news that State television was broadcasting a speech by the Crown Prince ordering the withdrawal of all military forces from the streets to allow a period of mourning for the victims before the start of dialogue.

The military vehicles and troops rapidly pulled out and the army issued Communiqué No.2: The withdrawal of military forces from the capital.

It was like a dream. The lumbering vehicles drove away to applause and shouts of joy as people leapt and prayed. 'We've liberated the square!' I tweeted proudly. I found myself part of this event, this lifting of the siege and together we sprinted for the roundabout, scarcely able to believe we had made it. It had been transformed into a true icon of the revolution; Liberation Square, Martyrs' Square, the Pearl of the Revolution, call it what you will, it was all of these things now.

The young protestors took their first steps on the grass amidst whoops of delight. Some knelt, some jumped around, embracing their friends, joking, chanting, giving thanks to God: moments only to be found in victory. And then, spontaneously, they began the task of cleaning up the square, gathering up the detritus of the assault that had disturbed their sleep two days before – hundreds of tear gas canisters, children's shoes lying scattered, toys, a doll – and everything they found was assembled in small displays dotted around the square. A group wrote out a message on the ground in stones that read, 'We love Bahrain and seek the interests of all its people'. In no time the square had become the scene of wild celebration, a crowd of thousands taking the Crown Prince's words as a guarantee of their right to peaceful assembly.

But it was this very assembly that they would pay for when martial law was imposed and the Peninsula Shield forces of neighbouring Gulf countries led by Saudi Arabia entered the square on 16 March. Everyone whose feet had stamped the square would be accused of treason, Persian sympathies and other indescribable slanders. They would be interrogated, suspended from work, fired, arrested, tortured or all of the above.

That evening the general secretary of the opposition and Shia Islamist Wefaq Party would take to the podium and address the tens of thousands gathered in the square:

> We don't want an Islamic state or a religious state; we want a modern, civil state, a state that can take its place as yet another icon of Bahrain's revolution and its pearl-like dream.

The regime would quite deliberately turn off its hearing to this claim. It would create another icon with which to poison the revolution's demands, falsely linking it to the Velayat e-Faqih (the Shia religious thought in Iran advanced by Ayatollah Khomeini), an accusation the protestors themselves dealt with when they said they has no intention of substituting one tyrannical regime for another. Moreover, the Wefaq Party had also stated that such a system could never be implemented in Bahrain.

The pearl of the square

I stayed late into the night, moving between the square and the cafes of Manama where debate raged and where I sat down to write an article about the martyred university student Ali Ahmad al-Mumin, the pearl of Pearl Square. The day's events coloured my words:

> Dear Ali, do you know that this evening, just three days after your passing we have not only broken the cup over your grave, but broken the very siege itself, here, in the place where you were assassinated. Over your body we read the first chapter of the Qur'an, the first chapter of our journey

back to the square. With you alongside us we widened Pearl Square and this evening it is larger by far than the patch of ground on which you stood exposed, defending it against the lies of the authorities. With your free blood we extended the boundaries of this square, this square so dear to us, its price not only your blood but your dream as well.

Did you not dream at dawn that day that a new sun would break over this square? Did you not hope that the spreading light would bring with it a new future for us all? Then the soldiers' bullets caught you unawares. They killed you, but fear not, they did not kill your dream of a Freedom Square. The pearl remained in our hearts; we sheltered in from the machines of war. Though they planted a bullet in your heart it never reached the pearl that you kept hidden and they never realized that you would return entire, a pearl in Pearl Square.

This is our first night after returning to the square that you never left. We returned to you; we returned with you. To you, because you have become the essence of this place, and with you, because you pursue us in our dreams, urging us on. I see you in every young man I meet. Your name gave them faith that they would return. The older generations did not believe; it was you and your comrades who gave them their faith, restored them to freedom's creed.

The next day I finished the article and it was published in *an-Nahar*, part of a special supplement on events in Bahrain. A number of Ali's friends and fellow students from the University of Bahrain copied the article and published it as a neat little booklet that was distributed in the square during a march by university students. Those who participated in this march were subsequently expelled.

A few days later I received a call. At first I did not recognize the voice, but when I did I lost the power of speech. 'I'm Ali al-Mumin's father,' he said and I burst into tears. I had not wept writing about his death. Two days later I was finally able to write the following on Facebook:

His voice took me unaware and I lost all self-control and the power of speech. He was thanking me for setting down his son's obituary in ink; I wanted to thank him for giving us a son who wrote the future of this country with his blood, but I could not summon even these words, nor did I have the courage to call him back because whenever I recalled the sound of his voice my own dried up. I've been trying to call him for two days now.

I would go on to meet his brother nearly a month later, after the passing of the 'National Safety Law' and the start of the Peninsula Shield operation. Our meeting took place at the funeral procession of Sitra's third martyr, Issa Ali, on 16 March. He called out to me in a voice in which happiness shaded into sorrow and introduced himself: 'I'm the older brother of the martyr Ali Ahmad al-Mumin. I've been looking for you to offer you my thanks.'

Writing about the encounter later, I broke down worse than before:

The world around you throbs and hiding your grief-stricken face you withdraw, bearing your woe, without a word of apology fitting to the occasion. I do not know how my heart can overcome the shattering sight of the dead laid out on the morgue's slab, their ripe young bodies offering up their ruptures as testimony. This heart of mine is powerless to protect itself when a father or a brother says to you: I am the martyr's father; I am his brother.

The square

19 February marked the start of a period of calm that lasted three weeks until the regime's hysterically violent response in mid-March. This hiatus and what came after would prove the real test for all concerned: for the opposition forces, be

they groups, associations or individuals, it probed at their diversity and helped define the limits of their common ground; it was a test of which kind of state (civil or religious, a constitutional monarchy or a republic) the crowds that bayed for change were hoping for; it was a test of how society would respond, the society that viewed this change as a pressing and inevitable reality; a test for the associations and organizations of civil society and their ability to interact with the revolution, the authorities and the people; it tested the credibility of the authorities' recognition of the rule of the people; finally, it tested the integrity of the intellectual's stance on common freedoms and the relationship between the people and the state.

The first outlines of a civil state began to take shape in the square. Anyone with a protest to make could find a place here: no one asked anyone about their affiliations or origins, their faith or creed. The square was a free space for the practice of free protest.

Some were the epitome of rationality and reason, some were wildly extremist and the rest lay somewhere between the two. No one was in charge of the square or its inhabitants; our only ruler was the flag of Bahrain that we saw fluttering so huge and high and proud for the first time. The further away from the centre of the square and the main stage the more diverse it got. There was a warm and non-judgemental welcome for you whoever you were, Sunni or Shia, Islamist or liberal, secularist, leftist or communist or simply a visitor from abroad. I saw the square as the wellspring of a new coexistence of a kind we had never before experienced.

At the liberal Waad Party's tent I set up camp, arranging to meet people, debating, discussing, and writing, too. It was there that I decided, along with a number of friends and fellow intellectuals, to produce a secularist liberal newsletter called 'The Square's Echo'. The first edition gave voice to the opinions and perspectives of the demonstrators, and 2,000 copies were printed out and paid for by Waad, whose party headquarters were first set alight then sealed up with red wax by agents and supporters of the authorities on 14 March.

In the newsletter we set out the demonstrators' demands and took them further still: a constitutional monarchy, the peaceful rotation of power and a fully empowered, elected parliament.

I held sweeping debates with my companions over what shape this diverse and plural civil state should take and was invited by the young activists of Waad and al-Minbar al-Taqaddumi (a leftist grouping, whose name means The Progressive Pulpit) to give a talk. The talk was delayed and then the forces of Peninsula Shield mounted their surprise attack.

Beyond sectarianism

A few days before this little oasis was swept away by the foreign armies, my latest book *Beyond Sectarianism* was released. On 12 March I tweeted: 'Today I received 37 copies of my book *Beyond Sectarianism* in dramatic fashion. I am barred from entering Saudi Arabia and my friend Abdel Wahhab al-Arid cannot enter Bahrain.'

How to get hold of the copies that he had brought from the printer in Riyadh in Saudi Arabia? We stood at the border; he gave me the books and I gave him my thanks and we each retreated inside the boundaries that are so much less than countries.

To my contacts, I wrote: 'I will be signing copies of my book on Monday, March 14, at the Waad tent opposite Palm Tree 6 in the Pearl Roundabout.'

The security situation began to deteriorate and tensions escalated. My book became irrelevant.

For that brief period, we had lived 'beyond sectarianism'; the roundabout, and all the diverse and conflicting factions that gathered there, had been an experiment in transcending sectarian division to dwell in a genuinely plural and open urban space. For this reason I thought it was the most appropriate setting for my book signing. Two days later, as the bulldozers levelled the uprights of the Pearl Monument, the army issued Communiqué No.6: the roundabout had been purged.

The roundabout had been seized by the tribe, who saw in it their own marginalization, and now, wiped from the map, it enters history.

That day we left the roundabout and entered sectarianism. We entered the sectarianism exploited by authorities jealous of their interests to eradicate the roundabout, and we left Pearl Square, which raised the call for equal rights for all without regard for sect, or tribe or faith. Amid the murk, it seemed that any degree of destruction would be permitted for the sake of holding on to power.

The square was a different way of life; it made you feel, as Palestinian poet Mahmoud Darwish once said, that there was something worth living for on this earth. I cannot see any meaning beyond the life fashioned by the Arab in his springtime, the life that has turned so many cities in the Arab world into squares of liberation.

This is a time that we will always be proud we were part of. We created it; we participated in. It is the great event of our age, our gift to future generations. One morning I sent the following message to all the Arab peoples going through their Arab Spring:

There is something worth living for on this earth. It is found in Bahrain's Pearl Square, Egypt's Liberation Square, Libya's Green Square and the Square of Change in Yemen.

And so it was that I made sure I was part of this event, part of this dream.

Beirut
July 2011

7

WISHFUL THINKING (SAUDI ARABIA)

By Safa Al Ahmad

'I'm Saudi. I'm sorry.'

It's a phrase uttered at every introduction in Tunisia, Egypt and Yemen, not so much in Libya. Whisper it to myself in Bahrain. As I walked into Amal's house in Sanaa, my friend greeted me warmly and apologetically declared she was boycotting Saudi products. She burst out laughing: 'Then I remembered I'd invited you over!'

The other guests were taking off their *abayas*, putting on make-up and relaxing after their long workday. 'Why are you wearing all black? Go put on something colourful!' Amal demanded of one of her friends. 'Look in my closet!'

'When will you have your own revolution so your government forgets about us?' asked Nabila. 'Do you need us to export some of our revolutionaries?' joked Belqis.

Although said light-heartedly, the words dealt a heavy blow, hitting a raw nerve I have been nursing for a while. The women were jovial, laughing loudly and greeting each other with hugs and kisses. Then we all went quiet and stared at Amal's newly acquired piece of art hanging on the wall of her *majlis*: a large painting of a little girl and a woman sitting sideways, each covered in a shroud. 'It means we are buried alive from childhood,' she said. 'Take it down!' shouted the women, 'It's too depressing to look at while chewing *qat*.' It was chilling: a bland light blue background and the two females covered in white, like ghosts.

We sat on low cushions in Amal's welcoming olive green living room, drinking milk tea, her cat purring from outside the window as it peered at us contently. I was trying not to swallow the *qat*, and just chew it instead. Holding a conversation while chewing is a talent I don't possess. We talked about the state of the Yemeni revolution, electricity blackouts, sex or lack thereof. I felt at home. Then another question hit me: 'So when will they allow women to drive?' A reminder, I was not at home.

Even Yemen, one of the poorest countries in the region, is ahead of Saudi Arabia when it comes to women's rights and civil society. Saudis often look down on Yemenis, see them as inferior. Sitting in a room full of intelligent, brave and independent Yemeni women talking about revolution, a real one happening on the streets, which ultimately toppled their dictator, it was evident they were decades ahead of us.

The entire Arab world was engaged in a collective uprising for its freedom and dignity and my countrymen and women were begging for scraps. Dancing around the edges of systemic problems facing the kingdom.

What do we want? Free political prisoners. What do we get? Killing, torture and, in the case of the Shia of the Eastern Province, shutting down mosques and Hussainiyas, disappearances and hundreds more put in prison for daring to ask what happened to their brethren.

What do we want? Women to drive. What do we get? Prison sentences and lashes, followed by patriarchal pardons. Then with a stroke of the royal pen, Saudi women were (maybe) to be given the right to run and vote for powerless municipalities, and the honour to be in the powerless advisory body, the Shura Council. Not enough? You may also work in lingerie shops. Rejoice!

People riled up over the crumbs that fall from the table. Storms in teacups. Nothing like sectarian and gender issues to get people distracted in Saudi Arabia.

Off with their heads! This is the government's message to all those who dare to speak out; even if they only tweet. This is the lesson the government wants its citizens to learn from these minor skirmishes.

***

To revolt against the ruler was to rise against your faith. This is what we were taught in school. 'Even if he's an alcoholic?' I was testing the limits of my teacher's patience. 'Yes,' she sighed. 'Even if he is a drunk.' Our religious studies teacher, fat, dwarf-sized, with short fake blonde hair, tried to reason with us. Better a leader who is not a perfect Muslim than chaos, which would inevitably ensue in their absence. So there were no circumstances under which Muslims could revolt against their leader? I couldn't believe what she was telling us. It was her fault. She was the one who had raised the subject. One moment it's 'those who don't pray go to hell' and the next you're being told to follow your leaders, no matter how nasty and un-Islamic. This was all abstract of course. No one, including the teacher, dared bring up examples. The teacher was serenely confident in her knowledge: 'If he errs, you may advise him in private,' she informed us. Then she looked straight at me: 'This chapter will be in the exam, girls.' In a country where the ruler is also the guardian of the faith, how can you have change?

***

I break into a cold sweat, cocooned in bed sheets with my hair sticking to my neck and my lucky necklace choking me. Sitting upright on the sofa I was trying to sleep on, I hear the rerun of Gaddafi barking the notorious '*Zenga zenga*' speech he had delivered earlier that night; the night before I was due to journey to Western Libya. I was sure it was going to be a massacre. I was scared, a low intensity, nagging fear of a stray bullet or worse: kidnapping or torture. I tried to talk myself out of going: 'So what if you were asked to go? Cancel!' I told myself with rising panic. I had no idea what I was getting myself into. Libya was a black hole in my mental map. Then a surge of happiness swept over me and tears welled up as they have done so many times this year: 'How lucky are you? What better way to get to know Libya?' I was living vicariously through others. The question settled and, charged up by my little pep talk, I jumped off the sofa and made sure that if I did die no dirty laundry would be left behind. A naive thought, I know. The living room looked as if a hurricane had passed through it. The electricity was cut in my Beirut apartment, and I had to fumble my way in the dark. I distilled my worldly needs into two small backpacks and headed to the airport. Libya was my third revolution so I had learned the importance of packing light: carry-on luggage and nuts.

Much like the disjointed political relationships of the Arab world, it proved impossible to find a direct flight from Beirut to Tunis and I had to get a connecting flight via Paris. It became clear that predictions of Gaddafi's quick demise were off the mark and driving to Tripoli was out of the question. Many journalists retreated, flying to Rome to take a connecting flight to Cairo, then spending 16 hours in a car to Benghazi. On the wall of what used to be the checkpoint at the Libyan–Egyptian border was written: 'Greetings from February 17 to January 25'. A grinning, armed youth offered us a steaming cup of tea. It would have been almost impossible for me, as a Saudi, to get a visa to Libya, but here I was, sipping tea on the border. I couldn't believe my luck.

It was raining lightly as we drove through beautiful green fields dotted with yellow flowers against the deep blue of the Mediterranean Sea. Of the few things I knew of Libya, its beauty was not one of them. Why hadn't anyone mentioned it before? Libya: crazy dictator, beautiful country.

'Where are you from? Really? So where's your hijab?' a man in Benghazi demanded to know, looking at me quizzically. Paranoia was rife in the first days of the Libyan revolution and everyone was suspect. As if being a Saudi is something you would want to fake. 'To each their own revolution,' I retorted, trying to be nice, but taken aback by his question. I was the only woman in the room, and for a second I wasn't sure what to say. I was offered a separate plate from the men at lunch.

Another fact not mentioned about Libya: as a generally segregated, conservative, tribal, oil-rich society, it had more in common with Saudi Arabia than its neighbours. Unlike in Tunisia, I spoke with a Saudi accent in Libya and had no trouble being understood, or understanding people. In the one Italian restaurant still open during the first weeks of the free Benghazi, the only people serving were two exhausted looking Egyptians and a nervous Bangladeshi. We had similar attitudes towards foreign workers who did most of our manual labour. They were essential to preserve our 'lifestyle', yet treated with a mixture of benevolent disdain or, worse, racism and outright hatred.

When at last I managed to get online in Benghazi, I found a petition demanding a constitutional monarchy in Saudi Arabia waiting in my inbox. The petition was initiated by Mohamed al-Tayyib, a well known activist from Jeddah. He has been making the same demand since the first Gulf war and has been jailed for his efforts. Over 600 people had already signed it. I closed my inbox. The day before, I had asked a very nice young Libyan revolutionary what kind of government he wanted after Gaddafi. With a straight face and no hesitation, he said: 'A monarchy'. King Idriss was a good man, he explained with a grin. We rebels already use the old royal flag. I got angry with him. How could he want a system that the rest of the Arab world was fighting to be rid of? Tunisia, Egypt, Yemen, Bahrain, Syria and Libya were all monarchies of a kind: a king who thinks he owns a country and wants to bequeath it to his children. In Saudi Arabia they even named the country after themselves. If

I have to feel like a piece of property passed down from royal father to royal son, then why would he voluntarily do that to himself? Where is the revolution? He looked startled by my reaction, but was adamant that it was the best way to govern a country in the Arab world.

The parallels with Saudi held even after a year of revolt, when another Libyan friend posted a questionnaire: 'Should the hijab be made compulsory in Libya?'

***

I was back in a hotel room in Cairo with full-onset revolution jealousy and depression. It was March 2011. The beautiful Egyptians had toppled the State Security Police, taking pictures, exchanging security files, crying in police stations and dancing on desks. It was intoxicating to watch. Their revolution was in such an optimistic phase at the time. Meanwhile, I was preparing to go back to Saudi. The much-anticipated Saudi 'Day of Rage' was a few days away. I logged onto their website and read their demands. The irrelevant and entirely un-revolutionary list included gems like '10,000 riyals minimum wage for every Saudi' and dire warnings of the threat posed to the country by evil Iran and the Shia. The issue of women driving was starting up again and I didn't think I could stand it.

The Shia of Eastern Saudi Arabia were out on the streets, but to demand the release of political prisoners, not regime change. No one had been killed yet, it would be months before that happened. People were being picked up in door-to-door arrests, low-key and under the media radar.

The night before the Saudi 'Day of Rage', I was sitting on the floor of a friend's house in Riyadh, feeling dazed and confused. Everyone was talking in loud voices about what they thought would happen, but not one of them was planning to attend the demonstration, or even be out on the street that day lest they be mistaken for a protester. The streets leading to the Ulaya Mall and other areas designated for the planned protest had been blocked off by police. Saudi security troops were out in force. Prince Nayif expressed his pride at 'his' people: the ones who had heeded his call not to demonstrate and those trusty religious leaders who deemed it *haram*. Good obedient people, they did what he expected of them, all except those pesky Shia.

***

That same March, they closed the bridge. They opened it. Only to Sunnis? Friends were turned back at the bridge connecting Saudi Arabia to Bahrain. Once upon a time, the only thing we worried about at the bridge was traffic. Now it's a sectarian interrogation. Will I pass? Should we boycott Bahrain? Saudis who used to go to Bahrain to shop, watch a movie or get a haircut suddenly found their getaway too heavy for light travel.

Mohamed was praying under his breath they would let us through. He didn't want to lose the fare I was paying him to take me over the bridge to Bahrain and back. There was traffic, but nothing compared to a regular weekend traffic jam. The queues at the Bahraini passport control were long and slow. On the window of each booth was a poster of King Hamad, the Crown Prince or the Prime Minister. There was tense silence in the car. I wanted to get in as well. I needed to see for myself. As he drove up to the booth Mohamed looked back at me and hissed, 'Act nice and smile.' That's how the other women passed through. If they thought you were Shia they wouldn't let you in. I was intrigued to see how they would work it out, since Saudi IDs don't have a category with this vital piece of information. On the window of our booth was a quote from the Prime Minister as a bumper sticker: 'We will not say: God forgives what has passed.'

A fat man with a thick moustache asked for our passports. He flicked quickly through Mohamed's Indian passport then settled back and slowly leafed through mine, proceeding to ask me a slew of questions I had never been asked before when crossing the bridge:

'Do you have family in Bahrain?'
'Do you have a Bahraini ID card?'
'Where do you live in Saudi Arabia?'
'Which city?'
'Which neighbourhood?'
'You last entered the country by air?'
'What country did you come from?'
'Where did you go next?'

I answered with a big smile. Getting up from his chair he says, 'I can't tell,' to another man in the booth. My eyes stung. He returned to his chair, looked at me with a smirk and said, 'Sorry, we can't let you in for reasons of national security,' as he continued to flip through my passport. I looked around at the other cars full of young men driving happily through. I'm the one who can't get in? I was indignant. Cocking my head to one side, I smiled and explained I was only going for dinner with friends in Adliya (a popular district of Manama full of bars and restaurants).

'I have a flight at dawn, I swear.' I almost showed him the ticket.

'You're flying from Bahrain,' he asked in alarm.

'No, no. Dammam.'

'You may proceed,' he replied, thinking he had figured me out. Mohamed burst into relieved laughter.

The bridge, King Fahd Causeway, unleashed every Saudi who had access to a car onto the tiny island. The trip was immortalized in a Saudi film called *500 kilometers* about a film enthusiast from Riyadh trying to go to Bahrain to go see his first movie in a theatre.

Bahrain was always more liberal, socially and politically, than Saudi Arabia. Forward thinking men would send their daughters to the island to study when there was no such thing as female education in Saudi, and many still do. Bahrain was Dubai. Hotels, bars and restaurants mushroomed, as did shopping malls, of course. For some of its inhabitants, this meant a rise of immorality. Stories circulated of local villagers stabbing staff of a nearby restaurant serving alcohol, and of riots and burning cars that shut down streets when Lebanese singer Nancy Ajram came to town and at New Year's Eve. In a tweet during the shutdown of the bridge and most of Bahrain, a protester echoed a sentiment felt by many: it was the first 'clean' weekend in Bahrain with no bars or nightclubs operating.

Green Saudi flags, joined at the base with Bahraini ones, fluttered on car windows and music blasted. It was 'Thank King Abdullah' day. People were out on the streets of Manama 'celebrating' Saudi's support for the Bahraini royal family in crushing the local uprising.

On my last visit to Bahrain in 2010 there had been a Pearl Roundabout, Salmaniya Hospital was free to treat patients, mosques were considered sacred and no one had heard of a Gulf Shield.

Sitting in the car, stuck in traffic down a side street, I saw a young man walking past a police station and taking pictures of the riot police in their full gear. They didn't like it. They told him to stop, but instead of doing what he was told the young man started shouting at them: 'You stop! Who the hell do you think you're talking to? You can't even talk to me in Arabic! You go home!' The police were frozen in place, staring at him in disbelief. I thought they would shoot him dead in broad daylight for his audacity. Who talks like that to twitchy men with guns? But they didn't do anything. They just stood there, mesmerized, and let him walk past, suddenly looking like scrawny little boys in ill-fitting space suits. The balance of fear had shifted before my eyes. They looked awkward and out of place. They probably did want to go home.

***

A rare meeting was due to take place, in April: Shia from Jeddah, Medina, al-Hasa, Dammam and Qatif were going to debate the state of internal Shia affairs in Saudi Arabia. I couldn't believe it and quickly asked if women could attend. Aside from issuing demands to stop protesting, I was curious to hear what the religious leaders were planning to do about the growing sectarian tension in the country. Under normal circumstances, I wouldn't have pinned my hopes on the outcome, but this year, I felt, a Saudi can dream. We drove to the house. Just ahead of us a police car was slowly cruising along, keeping an eye on the crowds of people making for our destination. The neighbourhood was full of haphazardly parked cars. We passed the patrol car and looked for a parking spot. Young men stood at the front door greeting people: 'Women down to the basement, then take a right. Thank you.' The courtyard was covered in a red carpet and there were tables of food for after the event. Men in white thobes and sheikhs in flowing black woollen overcoats and turbans were all heading down to the basement. A cameraman and photographer were on hand to record the meeting. Young men and women served Arabic coffee, dates and small sandwiches as people settled in their seats. People kept pouring in and more chairs were brought down from upstairs. By now, the spacious basement was filled with around 200 men and sitting behind them, 14 women.

The moderator opened with the words: 'This event was not properly prepared.' I choked on my coffee. In a long-winded, defensive introduction he explained that discontent was not peculiar to the Shia community, but was a feature of society in general. It was time to search for answers within the community. Bahrain was weighing on everybody's mind. Who was he talking to? After several empty speeches from the religious scholars who offered varying definitions of 'dialogue', its importance and its place in Islam, they ran out of time. Were they trying to drive us crazy?

Then, Dr Sadiq al-Jubran from al-Hasa spoke: 'The Taliban killed more of each other than the USSR managed during the invasion of Afghanistan. They didn't realize the importance of dialogue amongst themselves.' The room started to listen again. Next up was Sheikh Tawfiq al-Amer, an outspoken religious leader, who was one of the first to demand the government allow the Shia call for prayer in al-Hasa (it is already performed in Qatif). He had been arrested in February of 2011 after declaring his support for a constitutional monarchy from the pulpit and the protests for his release had been on an unprecedented scale in al-Hasa. I was looking forward to his speech. Out of everyone in the room he would surely break this chilling silence, this denial of the anger on the streets of Qatif and al-Hasa. He would put the rest of them to shame for their complacent attitude. Sheikh Amer decided to use his eight minutes to elucidate a verse from the Qur'an. He might have had a good point, we will never know. He ran out of time. The sheikhs were either utterly disconnected from reality or they did not wish to face it. They showed none of the courage events on the ground demanded of them.

For decades they have been one of the few channels of communication with the government, but this is changing. The Shia youth have found another way to push for their rights: street protests. The day before, a youth council had been formed to deal head-on with the problems facing Qatif. A young man who had attended both meetings described the difference: 'It's a well established fact that if you want a project to fail you put a sheikh in charge of it,' he said with contempt. 'We had a highly energized debate about what our agenda should be, how to organize, how often to meet and how many working groups are needed. It was a completely different spirit to this.' He shook his head in disbelief at how disappointing the sheikhs had been. 'Maybe this is a good thing. It will help move things forward faster,' he said with a smile. An hour later, I received a message signed by over 40 prominent sheikhs asking young people to stop demonstrating, and give the government a chance to carry out the reforms the Shia were asking for.

There were demonstrations the next day. And for a year to come, they would ebb and flow. Sheikh Amer was arrested a few months after this event and, at this writing, is still in government custody.

The rest of the country was silent. Looking east, to Bahrain.

***

In October, things changed. The government started using the phrase 'armed men', motivated by 'outside forces' to destroy the country. The accusation was that if you were Shia in Saudi, then your primary allegiance was to Iran and you were suspect. Communiqué No.3 after 2 November 2011:

> Due to what the population of Qatif is doing to attack national-al security and its men we have decided the following:
>
> 1. Electricity and water will be cut at 2am until all wanted men surrender to the authorities.
> 2. All salaries of the residence of Qatif will be frozen starting this month until the weapons are surrendered to the authorities.
> 3. The flag of the Islamic league and the Saudi flag on top of the Principality of Qatif show the people that the country is capable of stopping the violence and rioting in a brief period of time.

Communiqué No.3 is obviously fake, created to spread rumours and fear, and sent to many residents of Qatif during the crackdown on protests. By December, live fire killed six young men, first at checkpoints then at funerals. The sectarian divide between Sunnis and Shia is a sharp and deftly used tool in the kingdom, ensuring no coordination between the opposition on both sides against the regime.

***

I break into a cold sweat, cocooned in bed sheets with my hair sticking to my neck and my lucky necklace choking me. It is October 2011. I'm having a déjà-vu moment, I sit and watch Tripoli suddenly fall to the rebels. I watch the re-run of Saif al-Islam, looking crazed but free, outside the Rixos hotel after the rebels claimed they had captured him. It is the night before I'm due to go to Western Libya.

In the weeks following the fall of Tripoli, bodies were found all over the city: executed, bloated, cuffed and tortured. They were stuffed in fridges, buried in shallow mass graves, and tossed in ditches, cargo containers, valleys and garbage dumps. They were pulverized by grenades or left to bleed to death on hospital gurneys. You hear horror stories, but you rarely get to see them. Going back to a room with no running water after a day of death, I tried not to think about where my shoes had been. You block out the voices, the smells and the images and eat your tuna out of a can with crackers.

Standing in front of a mass grave in the outskirts of Tripoli, I tried to pick up my camera as they removed the fourth body from the pit. His decaying neck slowly gave way and the head nodded off, but was caught in time and held in place. A short young man shouted at me: 'You are not allowed to take pictures!'

I started to argue with him. 'Did Gaddafi call and tell you that? Who is giving you these orders?'

A group quickly gathered around him and he shrunk back. 'Everybody wants to be a Gaddafi now,' the Libyan next to me said angrily.

***

History, raw, unfiltered.

I am overwhelmed by the magnitude of what I have witnessed.

But I was just that, a witness. I stand in awe of what my fellow Arabs have achieved, wondering if anything close to what happened in Tunisia, Egypt or even Yemen would happen in my country. What would it look like?

'Close your *abaya*!' shouted a short man in his signature short white thobe, bright blue shoes and white high socks. He looked more like a fat, overgrown child with a nappy beard than a grown man. I was easily two heads taller than him and felt a strong urge to swat him away, but he continued to buzz around me. 'Close your *abaya*! I am from the Haya!' he exploded, declaring the obvious, that he was from the detested religious police, pompously called 'The Organization for the Prevention of Vice and the Promotion of Virtue'.

I gave him a look of disgust.

I was annoyed and confused. Why is this idiot following me? My *abaya* was not only closed but a bit too long and under it was a long white skirt and my hair was covered. Anger welled up, choked me, my hands started to shake, not from fear but repressed, bottled-up, festering anger. Saudi Arabia forces you to see yourself based on your gender. Living in Saudi is infantilizing.

I weighed my options between punching him in his expansive stomach, or continuing to ignore him. My anger grew as I walked. People I passed stared at me and then at something behind me. He was still in hot pursuit. It would have been a comic scene if it didn't have possibly dire consequences. I walked into a make-up shop and pretended to buy something. He walked in and demanded the sales person not sell me anything. My face burned. 'Do I look naked to you?' I burst out. He looked at me blankly, through me. I wasn't human to him, I was something to be despised, to be corralled, like sheep. Cover up and shut up. The so called 'religious' police did not deem me 'appropriate' and he had the power of the State, with which he could randomly humiliate and terrorize an entire population in the name of Islam.

'Close your *abaya*,' he barked again. He decided to call for back-up on his walkie talkie.

How advanced he was, using technology to enforce the most primitive of constraints. 'I will not talk to you! Where is your guardian?' he demanded averting his gaze from mine as I got into his face, shouting, 'Where is *your* guardian? Who gave *you* the right to harass me?'

I was surrounded by three religious thugs with crackling walkie talkies and hovering security guards, a reminder of how fast things can go badly in Saudi Arabia for no other reason than expressing yourself, speak up and they will try to intimidate you, crush you. And if you are female – your appearance alone is enough to get you in trouble.

People around me froze, staring. They couldn't tell if I was crazy or what the religious police were doing.

***

In August 2012, I was back in Saudi Arabia. On one of the main streets of Qatif, a white sticker is stuck on the blue street sign renaming it 'Martyr Sadiq Malallah Street'. Further down the road is graffiti saying 'I'm the 13th martyr', and a little ahead an arrow was drawn and above it read: 'Death to al-Saud' and 'Here, Flaifil was killed'. He was one of the first young men killed by the police. There is even a miniature Pearl roundabout. Dissent is everywhere.

The people of Qatif are angry, frustrated and split on how to get out of the quagmire they find themselves in. 'What do they think they are accomplishing with these demonstrations? Do they think they can topple al-Saud? Do they have a plan? A leader? No, they don't. Where does that leave us?' asked Om Abdullah, voicing her fears as I sat in her living room.

Since the demonstrations began, crime in the city had risen sharply. The robberies were becoming more bold, with thieves stealing not only from major shopping malls in broad daylight but then going on to rob a pharmacy or a clinic afterwards. For the residents of Qatif, the rise in crime meant that, either the government was neglecting its duty or it was encouraging it to punish the residents for the continued protests.

The Ministry of Interior had issued a list of 23 men on 2 January 2012 who were allegedly behind the demonstrations. Some of the names on the list were known criminals. 'Those who went out to demonstrate are unemployed men with nothing to lose. They are criminals and they are gay,' said Om Mohamed, repeating the rumours. She was from the now infamous Awamiya, a town close to Qatif and a source of many of the protests.

It was a joke during the revolutions that the Arab dictators were operating from the same handbook: 'In Case of a Revolution'. It said to call those who rise up against you criminals, terrorists, thugs, unknown gunmen and generally immoral drug users/dealers to alienate them from the rest of 'polite' society.

Even though no one wanted the status quo, few wanted to pay the price for revolt. Corruption, religious persecution and oppression were burning issues not only in Qatif but all over the kingdom. Yet only the Shia seemed to have taken to the street with such persistence.

Saudis wanted change, but were afraid of the unknown. What next? *Who* next? Is toppling the regime going to make things better? Or worse? And who is organized enough to take control?

2011 propelled dreams to reality, 2012 saw reality turning into a nightmare for the impatient. A Yemeni protester had shouted at me: 'We have been demonstrating for months! It only took the Egyptians 18 days!' as if a cruel joke had been played on him, and real change was a lazy worker who failed to show up to work on time.

***

I made arrangements to meet some of those on the wanted list from Qatif. Maybe they had answers. I wanted to meet those who were willing to risk their lives to go out and demonstrate. I wonder how they felt about being called criminals or gay?

I got in a car with a trusted friend during my last visit in August and we drove the few minutes it takes from Qatif through a checkpoint to Awamiya.

We passed through narrow streets and close-knit low houses, posters of Sheikh Nimr al-Nimr and graffiti filled with anger on the walls: 'Death to al-Saud', 'Down with Hamad' (in support of Bahrain's revolution). Sheikh Nimr was known for his passionate sermons against the government. But after the death of Prince Nayif, the Crown Prince and Minister of Interior since the 1960s, he didn't try to hide his dislike for the man in a public sermon widely viewed on YouTube. Although Sheikh Nimr had been a wanted man for years, his comments on the death of Prince Nayif seemed to be the last straw for the government. In a car chase, as the Sheikh tried to avoid the police cars and under a hail of bullets, he crashed. I was told by a witness that he was shot in the leg and beaten on the head with the butt of a gun. His car has been kept in the family farm near to where he was arrested and shot: covered and protected, as if a monument. It was carefully uncovered for me to see the damage and the blood, a testimony to the brutality of the method used to arrest an unarmed old man.

Awamiya is Sheikh Nimr's hometown, his family's home for generations. His grandfather and great grandfather lived here and were opposed to the surrender of Qatif to Abdel Aziz al-Saud, before Saudi Arabia was even a country. 'We are historically troublemakers,' remarked one of his relatives with a mischievous smile. His family was allowed to see him several times while he was in the hospital, but no one knew when or if he would be released. To date he is still in prison without trial. 'He asked us to vacate and return his rented apartment,' his relative said in dismay. I sat in the Nimr farm sipping juice as we waited for the green light and location to meet the 'wanted' men.

Awamiya was also the home of many of the most wanted.

The car passed slowly by a barber shop where one of the 'wanted' men was arrested as he was walking in. There are many informers in Awamiya, and the government arrests people at will. I wondered if we were being followed. The streets were quiet.

We passed a house decorated like a Christmas tree with a string of lights and a huge poster ahead of it announcing a wedding with the groom's picture displayed. A few metres away, another poster of Sheikh Nimr.

I walked through a brown curtained entrance into a small hallway, took a left into a matchbox room and sat on the first chair. Crammed on a sofa next to me were two young men, soft spoken, confident, calm. They didn't look as sinister as their Interpol mugshots. The younger of the two was sitting on the edge of the sofa talking animatedly with his hands. 'I wasn't involved in the demonstrations and definitely not one of the organizers, so I was surprised when I found out my name was on the wanted list!' he said with exasperation. 'After that I started to join, I thought that I might as well.' He even tweets. More of the 'wanted' streamed into the room, upbeat, shaking hands with each other. These are defiant men. When the list came out some had issued public denials of the government's accusations which included owning illegal arms, drugs offences and disrupting traffic. Hussain Rabih made a YouTube video showing the world where he lived: a little shack made of wood and corrugated sheets. Why are people living in abject poverty when there is so much oil under their feet he asked? There is an oilfield close by Awamiya, so this question is not an abstract one for them.

All the young men denied they had criminal records. One had recently become a father, but as a fugitive he couldn't register his newborn child.

They all agreed that the royal family must go. At first the demonstrations were about the 'forgotten', nine men accused of the Khobar bombings in 1997. To date, they have not even been taken to court. But after the killing started late last year the tone of the protests changed, became more extreme. Regime change seemed the only solution to some.

Do you believe you can overthrow the monarchy even though you are a minority? Do you have any other plans? These were hard questions to answer, they were aware of their limitations but insisted the monarchy must fall.

'They are zombies! They crawled out of their graves and want to rule us!' the eldest in the group declared with disgust as he sunk into the sofa. Those ruling the country are old, and the next in line are not that much younger. The question of succession is causing people to wonder who has enough power in the country to keep it stable. The last to walk in was a young fragile man whose father, an old man, was arrested last year in order to force his son to give himself up. This caused major demonstrations and a confrontation with the police, igniting the tensions once more. But if the young men were unanimous about their feelings concerning the royal family, they had conflicted feelings about the religious men who didn't support the Hirak, as they called their movement. Sheikh Nimr was one of the few vocal supporters. The conversation got heated and hours slipped by. I grudgingly had to leave, worrying about their safety and mine if we stayed any longer.

***

Sheikh Abdul Karim al-Hubail, a prominent sheikh of Qatif, was one of the few left engaging with the youth, but even he didn't go far enough for them. 'I feel like I'm swimming against the tide,' he said.

He cut a solitary figure, sitting behind his desk and fiddling with the coins in the drawer as he talked to me with his turbaned head bowed in concentration. 'This government has failed to deal with us as a state, it treated us as an occupier. They call us heretics and try to teach us about our heresy!'

Sheikh Hubail was indignant.

He was crushed with worry about the youth completely bypassing them in their pursuit of change. 'If the youth want no role for the religious men then they are calling for secularism, and that is unacceptable!'

But many of the youth feel the religious men failed them, I told him. 'Not only the youth! Even I feel that way,' he said, his head bowing even lower, suddenly intensely interested in the jingling coins in the desk drawer and looking at me only from the corner of his eye. He slowly returned to the conversation. 'There are around 2,000 sheikhs in the Eastern Province and none of them could agree on a unified vision.' So how do you see the solution I asked? 'We can't even agree on a vision to get to a solution!' Sheikh Hubail answered with exasperation. Prayer time came upon us and with it the natural ending to our interview, but I didn't get an answer. No one had the answer of how to get out of the vicious cycle the city seemed to be locked into.

Then on 26 September three young men were shot. One was a 16-year-old who was on the wanted list, the other two were his friends. Shot dead. One in the neck.

Sheikh Hubail decried the government's actions. He was held for interrogation for hours.

Both the Shia and Sunni religious men were shaken by the protests, not only the government. As more people rise up and defy the sheikhs on both sides, something that was unthinkable before for Saudi society has started to erode. Both religious establishments are no longer untouchable. The demonstrations and even the killings in Qatif and Awamiya pose no real threat to the government. The fear is in contagion. When the Sunni families do more than gather in front of prisons demanding their sons' release, and escalate their demands to something more focused on the government, this can't be explained away in sectarian terms. A national movement is needed, but no sign of it emerges.

***

Saudi Arabia, even though I was born and raised here, is a mystery to me. Its history grudgingly unfolds in fits. Very little is what it seems, events and motivations are cloaked in a multitude of 'interests' beyond the reach of the average citizen. When I first went to college in the States, I checked out every book I could find on Saudi Arabia. I was hungry for an 'unofficial' version of my history, hoping to fill in the gaps in my consciousness. More than two decades later I find myself returning to Saudi Arabia to fill in even bigger gaps. It's hard not to repeat history if you don't know it to begin with.

I went in search of a witness to the unwritten part of my history. Someone to explain, with more than a few pages, a monumental year in Saudi Arabia, when an uprising gripped the entire country. Abu Ali agreed to talk to me about his memories of 1979. He was a teenager then, but his affluent father had bought him a white Toyota Cressida. He used it to drive his friends to a big demonstration in Qatif. It was Ashoura and a revolution was taking place in neighbouring Iran. Spirits were high, and illegal flyers were stencilled and circulated to declare the uprising through Husainiyas and mosques in the city. 'We had no clear leadership, some of the religious men tried to stop the demonstrations, and few supported it,' said Abu Ali. It mirrored the current situation. We refused to say 'down with a person or in support of another', but 'down with injustice and long live freedom'. But events were not organized, and within a short period the National Guard arrived and killed the first protester. Diesel was set ablaze in the streets by residents to stop their advance. Hundreds were arrested and tortured, many went into exile.

The situation was much more dangerous for the Saudi regime that year, for the uprising in the East coincided with another much more lethal Sunni uprising in the West and an attempted takeover of Mecca.

Both were brutally crushed. And history repeated itself like a broken record. Scratching a looped tune of loss and desire for freedom.

8

AND THE DEMONSTRATIONS GO ON

DIARY OF AN UNFINISHED REVOLUTION (SYRIA)

By Khawla Dunia
Translated from the Arabic by Robin Moger

A woman appears on television and says: 'I'm the one who asked State security to come and take my son away; he's against the government and wants to go out and demonstrate. I can't control him: if he's with State security I know he's safe.'

A young man appears on television to disown his father, who runs a website that publishes details of events in Syria. As he speaks his tears fall. The smiling presenter says, 'They're tears of joy, because he's devoted to his motherland.'

According to State television, residents of the southern city of Deraa are demanding the army move in to rid them of the traitorous, destructive, Salafist, fifth columnists that live in their midst. So the army goes in and shuts the door behind them, leaving nothing but silence and checkpoints in their wake.

Actors, actresses and figures from the film industry implore the government to intervene to guarantee the provision of adequate nutrition and medicine for the children of Deraa, and are accused of betrayal and following foreign agendas.

***

We talk on the phone in whispers, trying to find some everyday language to convey what we feel, hoping that the person on the end of the line will get the message.

We are afraid that the phone is being monitored, that the house is being monitored, that our friends are being monitored. Is it time to leave the house, we wonder? Is it still safe to sleep sound in our beds?

Each morning we bid our loved ones goodbye as though it were the final farewell, and greet them again each evening as though they have returned from foreign lands.

***

We watch the alleyways, and the alleys watch us.

We watch the people thronging the street and they watch us.

We slip folded notes in wallets and books, perhaps waiting for the chance to raise the scrawled words aloft: *No to killing! No to sieges! Stop the massacres!*

***

We try to gather what information we can from bits of news scattered here and there.

We ask the taxi driver which roads are open and which are closed.

We switch off the phone and pull out the battery if we want to talk politics.

We observe the new cameras held by those we neither know nor trust, fearful that they might take our picture at a gathering in some public square.

***

We gather for prearranged demonstrations.

Our numbers are few. We withdraw, raising our eyebrows in greeting at others who are as disappointed as us, without having the courage to stand next to them.

***

Scenes which remind us of the republic of fear in George Orwell's *1984*, the difference being that the Syrian Republic is real and its rulers unleash still greater terror within its borders. For years we relaxed into our silence and oppression. We grew accustomed to it. It wasn't a problem for us. We would hear bleating voices from the flock and everyone would attack them and then, after years of prison or a voluntary repudiation of past indiscretions, silence would return.

We would laugh at strange and bizarre charges such as 'tainting the majesty of the State': after all, what was the State but a handful of individuals who had trimmed and shaped it till it fitted them as snugly as their own shoes? But such accusations return to haunt us in the moments we summon the courage to break the silence ourselves.

We used to call Syria the 'Kingdom of Silence' and it deserved the name. The 1980s were full of pain, a decade that saw the most widespread campaign of political oppression it is possible to imagine, directed against the Right, the Left and nationalists, as well as groupings sneezed up by the ruling party but distinct from it.

The 1980s are remembered for Hama – a city currently in revolt – where an uprising was brutally suppressed, tanks entering the city and homes and whole districts brought down on the heads of their inhabitants. At the time there was little sympathy for the doomed city, because the Muslim Brotherhood, which had declared a *jihad* to bring down the regime, did not speak for the majority of Syrians. The campaign against them resulted in the deaths of more than 20,000 citizens, not to mention the deportation and detention of many more, all of whom were treated with the utmost barbarity.

Nor were the Left and other opposition parties spared this treatment, destroyed by successive waves of detentions that lasted into the 1990s, muffling the Syrian populist, who, locking his pain into his wound, watched and waited for a moment of rebirth, like the present.

***

Syria has never been cut off from its Arab neighbours; in fact it has been as involved as can be in the region's problems, from Palestine to Lebanon and Iraq. Nor has it been cut off from changes in the Arab world. The Tunisian revolution, which sped by almost before we realized it had brought down the regime, was followed by the Egyptian revolution that Syrians, wounded as they were, engaged with and followed day by day until Mubarak stepped down. With all its pain and joy, we Syrians felt connected to their struggle. We envied what was taking place there, unable perhaps to credit that such events could take place here.

For every revolution there is a reason why they start and a reason why they escalate, and it was no different in Syria. The Tunisian revolution was started by Bouazizi, who registered his protest against social injustice by immolating himself. The Syrian protests were triggered by an extremely painful incident involving a group of children influenced by what they had seen of the revolutions in Tunisia and Egypt, and in particular the oft-repeated slogan 'The people demand the fall of the regime'. They were moved to scrawl these words on the wall of their school playground in Deraa, at which the security services arrested them and subjected them to brutal torture. All this might have passed unnoticed, had not the same security services scoffed at their families' demands to see them, prompting Deraa's residents to take to the streets in protest at the children's detention.

The inhuman treatment meted out to the demonstrators in Deraa, six of whom were killed on the first day of protests, on 18 March 2011, was painful. Yet even worse was the authorities' fabrication of a story of fifth columnists and Salafists to justify further abuse of the residents whose rage was intensified by the killings. Even after attempts had been made to mollify the town's inhabitants and the children released, the sight of their tortured bodies and torn out fingernails prompted further protests followed in turn by further suppression, then the entry of the army. Finally Deraa was placed under siege while the government refused to admit either the right to demonstrate or the deaths of any protestors, while promoting the idea of fifth columnists and an attempt to establish a Salafist emirate in the town.

All this led to the outbreak of demonstrations in other towns offering their support to Deraa and demanding an end to the blockade. Douma, a small town in the Damascus hinterland descended en masse into the street on the Friday of Rage, on 2 April, in solidarity with Deraa, provoking the authorities to open fire, thereby killing even more people whose deaths they refused to answer for, blaming armed gangs.

***

I myself experienced some of the confusion people felt towards events in Deraa. Syrians are not accustomed to take to the streets and demonstrate, given the existence of emergency laws that forbid it, on the one hand, and on the other, the existence of agencies of repression that forbid even the idea of it. Moreover, many Syrians support the authorities for various reasons, or are members of the Baath party who place their hope in the regime's new reformist policies. For these reasons, the demonstrations came as a surprise to many. It was as if they had been ambushed; as if it were impossible that what was happening elsewhere had made its way to Syria.

***

On that same Friday of Rage (2 April), a large number of people were killed in various parts of the country. Residents of cities throughout Syria decided to stand side-by-side with Deraa, to lift the blockade and discover just what had taken place there.

That day, I decided to go to central Damascus after hearing of a plan to start a demonstration in Marjeh Square. I met up with my friend about half an hour before the demonstrations were due to start and when we arrived what we found terrified us … In the centre of the square and around the Martyrs' Monument plain clothes security agents were ranked, no more than a metre between one man and the next, surrounding the area on every side. The edges of the square were crammed with police and security troops carrying electric batons and heavy wooden truncheons.

We walked on towards Revolution Street, heading for Hamidiyeh Bazaar. The street was full of buses filled with agents, who were watching passers-by and waiting for the signal to descend.

Hamidiyeh was almost empty, save for a few stallholders. The afternoon prayers had come to an end by the time we reached the Ummayad Mosque. A knot of people rushed out and we guessed that they were on their way to Marjeh Square. We noticed that the stallholders had started to gather up their wares and make for the side streets. Security was everywhere. When we got back to the square by the mosque we saw crowds chanting and holding up pictures of the President.

We asked where the worshippers were. Some said that they had been locked in after prayers to prevent them going out to demonstrate at the appointed time.

We decided to return to Marjeh Square. Perhaps the demonstrators had turned up. But nothing had changed. The buses still waited; the truncheons in the hands of the security agents seemed to have multiplied.

We didn't know what to do. We called friends of ours elsewhere in Damascus and it was the same for them as for us. But not everywhere. In some places the demonstrators were facing a tragedy. Near Kafr Sousa Square, the security forces shut the doors of the Rifai Mosque, trapping protestors inside. Demonstrators outside scattered, while security agents entered buildings around the square to prevent anyone from filming what was taking place or watching from the balconies.

Large numbers of pro-government supporters were deposited outside the mosque and they started chanting. They'd even brought a band with them, which clacked little wooden castanets in time to the chants.

The cameras from State television channels came to film the supporters. Once the scene had been rigged to their satisfaction, negotiations were opened to encourage the protestors to leave the mosque, but, fearful of what might happen to them, they announced that they would only leave with a guarantee of safe passage. This was duly given, backed up by the words of a senior State security officer: we're all patriots; everyone has the right to express their opinion; at the end of the day we've all got the country's best interests at heart.

Hearing this, the demonstrators emerged, only for State security, along with the organized gangs of thugs known as *shabiha,* to begin assaulting them with electric batons (the use of which is said to be proscribed under international law) and wooden truncheons. Then it was the turn of the buses, which were loaded with demonstrators before driving off to an unknown location.

It was a bloody day, which left tens of protestors dead. Most of the victims came from Douma.

***

The weeks passed calmly as news filtered in of arrests, funerals, prisoners being released and disappearances of activists.

After the tragedies of Deraa and Douma I thought of going to the latter on the Friday after the massacre. Visiting Deraa would have been impossible, given the siege and the curfew. In Douma, which was close to Damascus, it would be possible to get some idea of what was going on. For me, as for all Syrians, this was a matter of some importance. Did the armed gangs the government was talking about really exist? If they did, on whose behalf were they operating? Who was funding them? Who let them in?

Questions that needed answering and so we made up our minds, my husband and I, to go to Douma on the day they called the Friday of Steadfastness, 8 April.

When we reached the entrance to the town we were stopped by a roadblock manned by security personnel in plain clothes. One of them stepped forward and ordered all the passengers to dismount, cross to the other side of the road and go back where they came from.

Exploiting the fact that my husband is a doctor, claiming that he had come to treat a patient, we made it into the besieged town. We later learnt that the roadblock had been set up the night before to prevent anyone but local residents from entering.

Outside the mosque in central Douma a large crowd was waiting for the Friday sermon to finish. When it came to an end a pickup loaded with flags and signs pulled up and its contents were passed out. Some had come with their own signs, on which their demands were written.

I was a woman in a crowd of more than 30,000 men. Poorly concealed looks of astonishment from all. Some thought I was a foreigner; a journalist perhaps. But with a few exceptions these glances led to no more than curious inquiries.

We marched with the others. We chanted with them, mostly 'Allah, Suriyya, hurriya wa bass!' ('For Allah, Syria, freedom and nothing else!') and 'Hurriya ... hurriya ... hurriya ...' ('Freedom ... Freedom ... Freedom ...'), plus other slogans denouncing sectarianism. It was the first time I had heard 'freedom' chanted with such vigour and passion on the streets of Syria, without clubs or thugs or bullets.

An old man leaning on crutches caught my eye. He was walking along and chanting and the people repeated his words. He was extraordinary, with his imperfectly memorized slogans, his determination to interact with the others and give voice to the demonstrators' demands. Nor was the demonstration entirely devoid of high spirits: the calm atmosphere and the fact no bullets were being fired meant that everyone, from children to the elderly, could come out to take part. The whole of Douma was there. We had learnt that there had been negotiations with the authorities for a ceasefire in the town, and it seemed that the armed gangs had chosen to take a day off at the same time as State security, so there were no incidents worth mentioning.

On our way home we were forced to walk a considerable distance to take a taxi, which chose to wind its way through backstreets until we reached the outskirts of Damascus. There was a lot of talk in the taxi about events in Harasta, rumours that were confirmed when we finally saw a friend who had come back from the city. Intercity buses had arrived full of men dressed in civilian clothes and carrying weapons, who started shooting at demonstrators. Another group, also in civilian clothes, had attacked them with truncheons.

Tear gas canisters were fired.

There were other stories from other regions and cities that all spoke of clashes involving security troops and the *shabiha*.

That day the demonstrations were put down with great force, many were killed or injured and many more arrested.

***

The Syrian people are used to enduring their fears in secret, fearful of giving voice to them; they are used to letting their hearts speak without moving their lips. Syria is a country walled round with what the government refers to as safety and security, its justification for clamping its iron grip over every potential point of weakness, including journalism and the media, as if security is being offered in exchange for freedom in all its guises.

It was because of this iron grip, my lack of faith in the news being peddled by the local media (not to mention the melodramatic reporting of foreign news outlets, with their grainy videos of demonstrations that, it was said, originated in other countries and were then passed around as showing the truth of what was happening in Syria) and reports I had heard of events in Latakia and Baniyas, that I decided to go and find out the truth for myself.

I made up my mind to head west: first Latakia, Baniyas and Tartus, then on to Homs and Hama; a short trip to see, hear and feel what lay behind the words I heard and the obscure and fearful hints and gestures that came my way.

The trip from Damascus to Latakia resembled a journey from some novel set in a foreign land. I was with my friend Omar, who was originally from Latakia himself and who had previously served two years in jail on charges of Islamism. Omar shared my misgivings at rumours of Salafist involvement and the seemingly sectarian divisions that had started to appear between the city's Sunni and Alawite communities.

We little expected to have our curiosity answered on the highway that ran past Baniyas, but just before we came to the city we were informed by State security that we could go no further. After further attempts and two more roadblocks we pulled in at a bus stop and waited to be released.

It was here that we found out what had happened: following demonstrations calling for freedom and solidarity with Deraa, the city of Baniyas had lived through unforgettable days of fear and terror, the most recent being particularly fraught. Many of its residents had been killed, as had soldiers, yet nobody knew who had done the killing! The blame was being directed at armed gangs who had sprung into existence from nowhere, perhaps ready and waiting for this moment of chaos and disorder.

After the men of the city were arrested, along with the inhabitants of surrounding villages like al-Baida (which subsequently became something of a media cause célèbre after a video was leaked showing the young villagers being humiliated and abused by the army and security services) the only option left to the women was to take to the highway with their children and demand the return of their loved ones.

That's right. The women know how to stand firm and make their demands in a peaceful manner. The great thing was, no one knew how to deal with this manoeuvre of theirs. They were unarmed, so it was impossible to start killing them, and their only slogan was 'We shall not leave the road until the detainees are released'. They kept their vigil up into the next day and some of the men were returned to them.

Finally the passengers got off the bus, and we decided to take a car that drove us through winding streets, over the mountains and past Baniyas. In the hour and a quarter we spent in the hills we were stopped by 16 checkpoints. We showed our IDs at each one and patiently bore the looks of astonishment at our (most likely unanticipated) passage along the bumpy road through the villages.

Roadblocks belonging to the police, to State security and to the army ... and then more manned by members of the so-called 'popular committees', wooden staves in hand and hunting rifles resting by the roadside.

The villagers around Baniyas were plainly frightened, small wonder given the plethora of checkpoints at the way in and out of every village, but overall the treatment they receive is respectful and free of harassment.

Many of the scenes we saw at these checkpoints made us laugh: unemployed youth and retired old men finally with something to do (Operation Protect the Village!).

We left the villages behind and the road surface improved as we headed down to the Baniyas junction, from where the road split off towards Latakia and Jabla. Some of our fellow passengers said they didn't want to go anywhere near Baniyas: Why didn't they just wipe the city off the map and rid us of it once and for all! 'I hate Baniyas,' a young woman declared: 'How come we got landed with this awful place?'

Fed up with what was happening and dreaming of a return to a safe, secure world, people were bound to talk like this. The easiest way to rid oneself of anything different or unusual is to eliminate it; to pretend it never existed. To interact with it as an alternative opinion worthy of debate is something we have no experience of.

At last we had the highway to ourselves. The only cars we passed were all stopped on the other side of the road before the entrance to Baniyas.

Today I was proud to be a woman, like those unshakeable, strong women on the highway; happy to be in the company of people from the districts we passed through and share their fear of an uncertain future. My empathy even extended to the men of the security services and the army, constantly on the lookout for a stray bullet or sniper.

Yes: today I became a citizen. I cannot agree with those who want to wipe Baniyas off the map, or obliterate Deraa; I do not want another Hama, razed to the ground and rebuilt as a pliant, obedient city, desperate for peace.

***

Ever since I arrived in Latakia and hearing people's stories, I have been prey to uneasiness. I try to memorize what I can. I'm not brave enough to carry a pen and paper to scribble down my observations: I worry about my interlocutor's nervous watchfulness; his fear of the writing implements that constrict the words he wishes to speak without fear of censorship of any kind.

I let the words tumble out to the rhythm of flickering glances, twitching brows and hands. They bring me people's dreams.

Some will come true, some will not. Many fear their hopes will fall prey to discord and conspiracy.

I heard a lot of stories and a lot of reactions to them, as well. The stories tell of people's fear of civil strife, a fear that leaves them clinging to the promise of safety and security and those that can give it to them. They tell of a fear of groups at war with the popular protest movement, groups that are hiring foot soldiers and importing weapons, funds and false identities to set nervous hearts aflutter.

I heard about growing sectarianism, jingoism and of the threats and accusations of betrayal received by those who had tried to fight it.

I heard of those who had been killed over the course of the past weeks and of the fear that had followed the killings; of residents unable to place their homes in mourning or write the names of their departed on the walls.

I heard of neighbourhoods blockaded by the army, with the help of security troops and anonymous bands of men who seem to have descended from another planet.

I heard of dozens of injured people who, despite their wounds, were beaten and accused of being traitors.

Yes, there were a lot of painful tales: live rounds fired at demonstrators, snipers on the rooftops; phantoms terrifying the safe and secure. There were attempts to mollify, then attempts to terrify. Agents! Fifth-columnists! Traitors of every stripe; heroes of every hue. Breasts bared while throats cried freedom, families sleeping hungry, schools closed because teachers were too frightened to come and open them.

Some neighbourhoods are defined on partisan grounds, others for other reasons. These classifications are common currency, recklessly inflated to conjure up a ghoul: a ten-headed monster that will descend on Latakia's residents and gobble them up whole.

***

15 April, the morning of the Friday of Persistence: the day that people from all sides have been dreading.

Today we marched down roads through neighbourhoods where the demonstrations usually take place. There was a big security presence. The army took over many public squares and thoroughfares and there were security troops accompanied by strange-looking men carrying outlandish weapons.

Between the start of Friday prayers and its end, Latakia hung suspended, swaying between attempts to secure food supplies and the expectation of what might happen.

There are those that say it will be calm: the demonstrations won't happen today.

There are those that say no one will have the guts to take to the street.

There are those that say anyone who goes outside will be wiped out.

Then there are those that prefer to keep their eyes open and see what happens.

The fear that some feel towards the demonstrations making itself felt in the form of pleas from friends not to go to those areas declared out of bounds by the authorities. Some advise me not to go, while others decide not to leave their homes. Yet more say they're too old for the protest movement. Some, though, choose to take to the streets to find out what is happening.

Posters and signs have been set up throughout the city's streets, cautioning against civil strife, calling for brotherhood and lecturing us about division and sectarianism. We have heard more about this sectarianism from the State media in a month than we hear from ordinary people in the three neighbourhoods we have marched through. 'Division! Division!' Until the concept is firmly fixed in the people's consciousness and they become watchful and fearful of the person who was just recently a friend, a neighbour or a lover.

The bullet whizzed past my ear, and I don't deny it: I felt the fear of those around me as my heartbeat quickened and I tried to take a picture with the camera-phone I never took out in public.

Some people told me to come and hide in their home. I was a stranger in a strange city, standing in the middle of a strange street, at a demonstration surrounded by strangers. Fear brought us together, uniting us in the face of the onrushing unknown.

I peered from the window, watching the progress of the extraordinary and fearless young men in the street. Young men yearning for freedom.

With the women of the house I jumped in fear at the stray bullet, fired by a sniper with an unfeeling heart, or perhaps an envious eye, who picked off anyone who leaned their head out into the street, or dared to carry a phone or camera in public.

Today I took a photograph of one of the dead. He took a bullet in the head. I didn't know his name. I heard there were more wounded and injured that I didn't see. I also took pictures of the demonstrators' determination to carry on, reorganizing themselves and entering the side streets to finish what they had begun.

From the windows we watched large vehicles move down the street. Armed security troops gathered around and got in, leaving the doors open and their guns hanging out. They were followed by pickup trucks carrying bizarre-looking men with black masks over their heads and automatic weapons in their hands. They were sitting on the back of the pickups pointing their guns at the buildings. A sniper stood in the middle of an alley between two buildings his eyes flicking back and forth as if he were trying to get a bead on the fly buzzing about his head.

The woman asked me to stop taking pictures. 'They'll see you,' she said. 'Don't put all of us in danger.' I could think of nothing to say, and I obeyed her.

I waited a couple of hours and when movement began to return to the street after the armed curfew we had just witnessed, I said goodbye to the homeowners and went out into the street. All the way back, down the long road packed with soldiers and security troops, I tried to outpace the terrible memories of what I had seen.

***

On 16 April, the President gave a disastrous speech in which he accused everyone who had taken to the streets of being traitors and divided the population into two camps: with me or against me. Afterwards, people grew afraid of what might follow these words. Even his supporters weren't expecting it and they found themselves unable to defend his speech: he had not mentioned the dead nor paused for a moment's silence in memory of the fallen.

Coordination committees began to spring up in the street, composed of young men from the neighbourhoods who prepared for the demonstrations that were to be held the coming Friday.

I met a number of these fervent young men. All week long they dreamt up alternative forms of action: how best to express solidarity with the besieged cities and how best to make their voices heard abroad given that the internet was likely to be cut off and given, too, their fear of leaking images via the web and subsequent arrest.

***

Conspiracy … Division … Conspiracy … Division …
The State media continues to strum the same old tune, and there are those that listen. Some people have even boycotted so-called anti-government channels, content to get their news from Syrian television and radio alone. Large swathes of society have chosen to keep silent about the crimes being committed. Others praise these crimes as a war against Salafism, or armed gangs, or those who seek to return Syria to the Dark Ages, and choose to ignore the fact that there are many people who stand behind the protestors' demands, which are now beginning to crystallize, growing more forceful with every passing day.

The Syrian state media is truly pitiful, and that goes for the so-called independent outlets as well. This independent media is owned by current or former regime figures and has toed the line. Videos and hastily snapped pictures exposing the abuses of the security services continue to be leaked abroad, enraging the authorities so much that they have started shooting at anyone holding a mobile phone or camera. That's right: people have been martyred for a photograph.

For a brief moment it seemed as if everyone would turn their backs on the protestors. A number of intellectuals and former opposition figures sided with the regime, some drawn by the idea of Salafism and the danger it posed, others simply preferring to be on the winning side. The majority kept quiet and looked on nervously.

Fear at what was coming was rife amongst Syrians. When the regime called on its supporters to take to the streets, more than ten million showed up! It was a truly extraordinary figure, and might have proved an insurmountable obstacle to the opposition. Yet anyone who knows the Syrian people, knows that the number of people on these pro-regime marches is not an accurate reflection of reality.

The Syrian coast is where the regime enjoys most support. The government considers it a special region and permits no one to meddle in its affairs and the mounting difficulties it has been experiencing at the hands of the shabiha. The shabiha have been around forever on the coast and their power and the gang-like structures they use to gather funds, intimidate and operate weapons, drugs and people-smuggling rackets, affects everyone. The gangs are run by members of the ruling al-Assad family and their close circle. No one dares cross them: the result would be death, mutilation or exile. The only possible response is silence.

Hence the shabiha's dogged determination to stop any attempt at protest by any party at all. They took to the streets in shows of strength, firing off rounds and spreading fear, not to mention murdering people. One of the stranger sights one can see at a demonstration is the army and police pulling back to make way for the shahiba when they arrive.

Nobody has the upper hand as yet, but the situation as it stands is deeply worrying and it is impossible to predict what is around the corner.

***

Will we really have to endure more pain after a day like today?

Are we to be reborn in this instant, fragmented, divided and marginalized, like chess pieces unable to leave their square without the player's helping hand?

I had no inkling how cut off in my square I was until these last few terrible days. I carry within me the terror on those raw untested faces that brought me to a halt before the tragedy in the street. Standing at the limits of my chess-square I stopped and returned to the centre. The player had spoken: my turn to move had not yet come.

I go home. Home is the sanctuary of the upright citizen. Home is the woman's kingdom. That's what they used to say. Today, it's the kingdom of everyone who has no stake in the game being played out by the powerful.

I leave the neighbourhood of Somariya and start to head home. Somariya is commonly seen as the dividing line between the city and the countryside and was built by Rifaat al-Assad (uncle of Bashar) for his followers who spent their time oppressing and terrifying ordinary Syrians. After he left the country it became one of the worst neighbourhoods in Damascus, a place surrounded by slum-like zones that housed his retired thugs and their children alongside recently arrived rural immigrants. The main road is lined with stores peddling smuggled goods whose owners and operatives are protected and employed by senior police officers. Every kind of contraband can be got here: booze, tobacco and foreign foods; even drugs are sold under the table.

For those who live in the suburbs one has to pass through central Damascus: the forbidden zone. The idea of a rural revolution seems terrifying today. How terrifying must it be for our fearless intellectuals?

Imagine! The desire for rejection and change welling up in the peaceful, passive and beautiful Syrian countryside, invariably depicted as a cheerful, active man, mattock in hand, wrapping his headdress about his head and gazing proudly up at the sky.

Yes, that very man, carrying that very mattock, but now he has taken off his headdress. He has laid it aside and he will only take it up when he can wear it with dignity.

Is this the beginning of a split with the intellectuals, who will now fall behind the rest of the population, as they always do?

I leave my peasant and his mattock in one corner of my thoughts and stare out at the row of tanks to my right and the soldiers surrounding them. Every alley in Madamiya was blocked by a tank and two or more scowling infantrymen. Madamiya is located next to the Qatna Road and was once a mainly rural district, with endless fields full of crops. Large areas have been turned into military barracks, while others have been used to build residential blocks for officers from the armed forces and the police. The original inhabitants were never compensated for the loss of their land, and this is one of the reasons the poor of Madamiya rose up against injustice and persecution.

I see a woman handing some bread and cheese to a scrawny soldier standing at the crossroads outside her house. He nibbles at her gift and smiles at her child.

Another soldier sprawls on a chair with some young men from the neighbourhood he is guarding.

What battle is going to take place here? Where is the enemy? Why are they sprawled out like that?

The scene is confusing, the enemies obscure, the battlefield uncertain. A single side engaged in a conflict with an unknown foe. No one knows the identities of the fiends who will take the field against these soldiers.

Today, in the passage – my passage, which I walk down every day – I am stopped at a checkpoint. 'Give me your ID.' A pointed command, directed at me by a youth yet to start shaving, with a truncheon in his fist and a cigarette tucked behind his ear like a man of the world.

I hand him the ID. There's no space for refusal here. Protecting residents from the separatist devils is a matter of life and death.

I relax back into my normal walk. I enter the house. I think: I must get a new steel security gate, plus some iron bars for the windows and balconies. It's a project I have been putting off, but now it's a necessity.

I open the window and turn on the television. The battle against the devils goes on. I take myself off to another corner of the wonderful world of television. They are talking about cities under siege.

Cities under siege …

Deraa is besieged; the city of the peasant who laid his headdress aside in protest at his children being tortured in prison. What kind of heart sits within me, that fails to tremble at the word siege?

Baniyas, al-Baida, Latakia, Homs, Douma, Harasta, Qamishli, the blockaded alleyways and lanes of Madamiya that I left just a short while ago.

How hard it is to talk of a heart having chambers.

To be a green olive branch in the hand of a demonstrator felled by a bullet in your streets.

To be a young man rejected by others, your death denied just because you are different.

To be accused of ruining people's day – their livelihood – merely because you chose change at the moment of change.

How confused and muddied it all seems, in our hearts as in our streets.

The situation is sad, depressing even. Worse, it is a recurrence of a scene we all watched and believed in when it took place in another country, though now, because it's happening to us, we do not want to believe.

***

After more than two months of protests we are still watching and waiting. The protests reached Homs. Bizarre things took place there: some demonstrators tried occupying the city's main square but were fired on.

On 18 April, the demonstrators valiantly fought off the authorities and after lasting out seven hours in central Homs, many began to feel cheerful. But they were violently dispersed in the end, and many of those in the square shot at. We heard that more than 200 of them were killed there, but it was impossible to be certain: dozens were missing and injured as well.

The districts surrounding Homs, in particular the city of Tilbeesa situated along the main highway, witnessed bloody demonstrations that were savagely put down, with the army intervening. Likewise in Rastan, which had demonstrated in protest at the siege and repression. Inhabitants of the city pulled down a statue of former president Hafez al-Assad on 15 April, thereby increasing the violence used against them when the army moved in.

Given the silence of the State media over developments we didn't hear much. We were told that fifth columnists and gangs were terrorizing the people, and given the tanks and soldiers we were unable to enter the besieged cities ourselves. The silence seemed to hang over many of Syria's besieged cities.

There were rumours in Homs of vehicles cruising through neighbourhoods and spraying fire randomly into the air. Fears of sectarian conflict grew. Residents stopped walking the streets at night and kept a wary eye on what was happening.

For some, entering the neighbourhood of another ethnic or partisan community became impossible after the brutal slaying of an army colonel, Abdu al-Talawi, along with two of his own children and a nephew, as they left their house on the morning of 18 April. The first symptoms of vengeance began to surface amongst frightened citizens. The authorities made no effort to respond to the crime, quite the opposite: State television showed close-up footage of the bodies that filled the screen for hours at a time, which so enraged government supporters that some took to the streets with knives and hatchets looking for revenge.

Blood. Revenge. The media fomenting strife and the authorities maintaining their silence. No voice can be heard above the gunfire.

And still, despite it all, Homs jokes.

Homs is famous for the sense of humour and light-heartedness of its inhabitants, and they have responded by making fun of the situation. A man asks a passer-by the way to his friend's house. 'See the first tank?' he says. 'Go past that one, then the one after it and when you get to the third tank, turn right. You'll see a security agent. He's standing next to your friend's house.'

***

In spite of everything I still insist on calling this Syria's moment.

Syrians, who have lived under emergency law, customary law and exceptional law for 50 years, are for the first time mobilizing en masse in cities and districts throughout Syria. In the course of 40 years Syrians have suffered imprisonment, persecution and exile, others have been murdered or have disappeared. After living in fear of the State security agencies they are defying their rulers at last.

As many young Syrians go out to demonstrate, they are trying to understand the history of tyranny in their country and what it means for them. We used to say that the youth were apathetic and selfish, interested only in the internet and the siren call of the West.

Of all the things that are happening in Syria today, these young men and women are the most astonishing. The coordination committees created by the protest movement in a number of cities are mostly comprised of young or middle-aged men trying to create a bridge between their slogans of civil society and citizenship and a young generation that had no understanding of these concepts. We saw crowds of youth chant slogans in support of freedom, unity between different communities and ethnic pluralism.

The authorities, on the other hand, have sought to divide Syria into its constituent parts leaving it as chequered as a chessboard. Tanks, soldiers, State security and the *shabiha* have encircled volatile areas, preventing anyone from leaving or entering and severing all channels of communication and means of knowing what is happening inside. Phone lines, water and electricity have all been cut off from the besieged areas.

They want to turn the country into an archipelago of disconnected islands, to prevent Syrians from sympathizing with one another, enabling them to exercise control and put down the protests. Yet many in society have refused to accept this: men and women; boys and young fellows in the flower of youth. This should come as no surprise. For the first time we feel that we are citizens, bound by one umbilical cord to our mother, Syria.

***

Despite the siege, thousands of Syrians continue to take to the streets, breasts bared to bullets, brutalization and arrest. All their inventiveness is required to keep up the protests, if only for a few minutes.

Two demonstrations by women were held in the centre of Damascus and some of the women detained for a few days.

At another demonstration a number of young men and boys were arrested singing the national anthem and holding signs demanding that the siege be lifted, the killers brought to account and a halt to the use of live rounds against protestors.

My husband was arrested at this demonstration.

Dear God! A thousand images crowd in on me.

This is the third time my husband has been detained. The first time he was held for more than eight and a half years on a charge of belonging to a banned party. At the time no time limit was set on arrests or convictions, and one could be held for many years without trial or sentence. The second time was for a few months, and since then he has been banned from travelling abroad. Today I am more worried for him than I have ever been, because this time it seems to be a matter of taking revenge against the demonstrators.

For three days, whenever I saw footage of his arrest on television, singing the national anthem in the street then roughly shoved into a security vehicle, a tear trembled in my eye. I don't know why. I knew this was coming, either for me or for him.

Well it was coming, and it came, but it chose him first.

I got to see him three days later after he was transferred from the State security building. He looked awful: his eye swollen and his shirt ripped. His clothes practically slipped off him he was so worn out and skinny. What did they do to him? I felt an urge to run from the sight. He was crammed in with dozens of other prisoners, some of whom I knew, and none in better shape than him.

Looking at him, terrified that my tears would suddenly pour down without warning, I muttered something and left.

After a week in prison he got out on bail. The charge was demonstrating without a licence. The marks of the beatings were still visible on his body. The torture had been brutal, if more bearable than what others had experienced in Syria's outlying cities, the evidence of their corpses on State television speaking eloquently of what they had suffered in the cellars of State security.

***

I'm for calm debate. I never champion one side at the expense of another. All I want is the truth. I want the killers to be tried regardless of what side they're on. We need people to calm down, but who do we speak to? The regime? Whoever's playing with people's lives? Some say the protestors need to stop demonstrating, but everybody, the regime included, admits that the demonstrators are peaceful. So where's the problem?

People are being asked to stop the demonstrations on the grounds that it causes bloodshed.

Today in Deraa the situation escalated further. There was talk of asking the residents to stop demonstrating, as if that might bring a halt to the bloodbath or prevent the armed gangs, fifth columnists and Salafists from taking advantage of the situation.

I don't believe that I or anyone else can judge what is right for the citizens of Deraa and the other besieged cities, were they to choose to stop demonstrating after all this blood has been spilt.

Yes. Now, it seems, it is imperative that we put pressure on the regime. We must make it change its policies towards the people, otherwise Deraa will be transformed – as a leading figure in the regime has boasted – into a potato field, and Baniyas into a building site. And I have no idea what is being planned for Homs, Aleppo, Qamishli, ar-Raqqah and all the other cities that have risen or will rise against the regime.

***

Fear of foreign intervention, along the lines of what happened in Libya, is now doing the rounds. The demonstrations have now spread over most of Syria, joined by new cities and social classes previously too timid to take to the streets. The authorities' stubbornness, their lack of desire to enter into dialogue or make concessions, has prompted Syrians to come up with their own hilarious interpretation of events. The regime's attitude towards foreign intervention is like that of a man who beats his family. He flogs his kids while his eyes shoot sparks at disapproving neighbours. Furious, he screams: 'Feeling their pain are you?

Your hearts bleeding for them? Why? It's because they're your little agents, isn't it? You've left your prayers to come and goggle at me and my family. Well, I'm free to do as I like: I hope they die and there's nothing you can do about it! Get out of here!'

Then he turns to the mother who is weeping and pleading with someone to come and help. 'Asking strangers to get involved, you traitor?' he roars. 'I'll burn them alive and break your heart, and when they're done I'll burn you, too! Traitors! Dogs!'

***

Three months into the protests and the picture grows ever more complex, but still there are little victories. Each new Friday makes its mark in Syrian history, none more so than Azadi Friday, the Friday of Freedom, on 20 May. This is the first time a Kurdish word has been trumpeted so proudly on Syria's streets. I can understand the joy of Kurds, who suffered persecution for many long years and were treated as second-class citizens.

'*Azadi! Azadi!*' – 'Freedom! Freedom!' – the demonstrators roared, and so more of them fell. It was a Friday that they announced that Syrians of all ethnicities and groupings had found their way to citizenship and the civil state. Blood had united them as never before.

Talkalakh is a city in the Homs governorate close to the Lebanese border. It joined the ranks of the demonstrators and offered up a fresh batch of dead. Residents fled to Lebanon and the army entered the city as regime loyalists scattered rice on their tanks.

There was a Friday (27 May), labelled 'Guardians of Society' named for the Syrian army in an attempt to break down the barriers that separated the protestors from the common soldier, many of whom have died in clashes or been executed for refusing to open fire on demonstrators. These soldiers, who have embarked on a war against the demonstrators alongside the security troops, the police and the *shabiha*, seem utterly powerless, unable to choose between carrying out orders and their own deaths.

The State media remains coy, continuing to insist that all is well. Things are being brought under control. Armed gangs were behind the killing of demonstrators, soldiers, officers and security personnel. The death toll amongst civilians rose above 1,100 in addition to unknown numbers of soldiers and security troops.

In areas with ethnically mixed populations, fear of sectarian conflict rules the field. News reached us in the shape of rumours: slayings, vengeance, corpses put on display.

Those who support the authorities are vehement in their defence. We heard of joyful ululations in certain districts when tanks rolled into neighbourhoods belonging to a different community.

Where is the country heading? The future is terrifying and obscure.

I was forced to leave my house in fear of being arrested and I cannot be sure whether this might still happen to me. Many others have also left their homes, especially activists and those who have appeared on Arab and foreign satellite channels to talk about events in Syria. The fear of arrest took hold after many opposition figures, activists and journalists were detained, a campaign that included taking hostages for those who weren't at home.

The authorities put about the idea of a dialogue with the opposition, but without setting out any basis for the dialogue or defining who is to take part. The Syrian opposition in exile, from the extreme right to the left have decided to hold a conference in Turkey. There are a lot of questions and mistrust about this conference within Syria, especially from the coordination committees who are the ones active on the ground.

From Fridays, where people are killed, to Saturdays, where more people are at the funerals of Friday's victims, the demonstrations now take place all the days of the week.

Sanctions are enforced against a group of leading figures, at their head the Syrian president, and bank accounts are frozen. It's a move that seems to carry little weight in the calculations of the authorities, who persist with their stubborn course, giving out no hope of a solution to the crisis and making no concessions to the demonstrators and their demands.

There is footage of the child Hamza al-Khatib, a 13-year-old from the municipality of Jeiza in Deraa, who had been barbarically tortured in prison. He had been detained at a security cordon in Houran on 29 April after leaving Jeiza to help raise the siege around Deraa and was handed back to his parents almost a month later on 28 May, a lifeless corpse with scars from torture and bullet wounds visible on his body. This provokes the ire of the opposition: more demonstrations are held; loyalists grow ever more afraid of partisan revenge.

The footage proves that the Syrians' revolution is really one of transmitting images abroad. It is the revolution of the mobile phone versus the bullet.

I decided to travel to Homs to find out what had happened there, so I won't have the time to give you an idea of what will follow from the Syrians' struggle for citizenship and the civil state.

***

Today, 23 June, marks 100 days since the start of the Syrian uprising. Dear God, what days! More than 2,000 have been killed and upwards of 15,000 arrested. Thousands are missing and tens of thousands have fled across the borders with Jordan, Lebanon and Turkey.

The refugees who crossed from Jisr al-Shughour (from 6 June) and other border regions into Turkey have received the greatest share of the media's coverage. Jisr al-Shughour is a small district in the northern province of Idlib on the Turkish border. Its population of 45,000 has lived through two massacres in recent memory. The first courtesy of Hafez al-

Assad and the second the work of his son, Bashar, in 2011. Rights organizations and eyewitnesses stated that no less than 70 people were shot down by Syrian security forces, who then cut the city off. Residents reported a heavy military presence in the city, constantly hovering helicopters and widespread domestic raids to detain civilians and search houses. Images on YouTube show a city of ghosts left behind after residents fled to Turkey in fear of the regime and its loyalists seeking revenge.

What will become of the uprising after Jisr al-Shughour? It is a critical question at a critical moment. How long can the protest movement remain peaceful in the face of all this thuggery?

Divisions have begun to appear in the lower ranks of the army, but the regime still possesses the strength to send its tanks into the remaining cities in the north and east of the country.

And the demonstrations go on, the daily cycles flaring up on Fridays, which each bear different names sometimes designed to excite the enthusiasm of those that remain silent on the sidelines, sometimes to draw attention to a particular issue, and sometimes to affirm the values and goals of the revolution.

We start to detect a political discourse taking shape within the movement inside Syria, while the traditional Syrian opposition abroad continues to convene at conferences that do no more than declare support for those at home.

In those cities that have nearly managed to liberate themselves from regime control the revolution diversifies and blooms. We hear of creative attempts to interact with security troops, of singing on marches and of jokes about incidents that take place here and there.

The young revolutionaries display great inventiveness in getting information about the revolution abroad despite the internet and phone networks being shut down in the besieged cities.

The economy is in bad shape and heading for collapse, and we see tentative concessions accompanied by ambiguous talk of a national dialogue and economic and political reform. It is clear that the regime is staggering a little from its exposure before the eyes of the world and the increasingly punitive measures adopted by the United Nations.

But it is still too early to talk of its demise.

Amid all that has happened and still happens there are things we must thank the regime for. Today, for instance, we are closer to one another than at any time in the past. Our motivation to press on until we achieve change is stronger than ever. Our mission now is to restore the faith of those in society who are now more frightened than ever of what tomorrow brings, of those who fear the revenge of the regime's allies, and of those who historically have been exploited to strengthen their rule. This means going into the street and engaging with people directly.

We meet with political parties, youth and religious leaders of all stripes; we initiate wide-ranging debates about the movement and how to help it evolve and be more effective. There is consensus over the goal of a civil state.

***

On 20 June, the President gave a speech in which he put forward what look like concessions. They satisfy nobody. At the same time, as if emphasizing his earlier message, he tells people that either they are with him or he will continue to wipe them out. The decision to keep demonstrating is a given: directly after the speech protests break out anew.

My faith in the future is huge. Although the sacrifices are great I feel optimism. I feel optimism that these sacrifices will not be for nothing.

And the demonstrations go on, into the unknown.

Damascus
July 2011